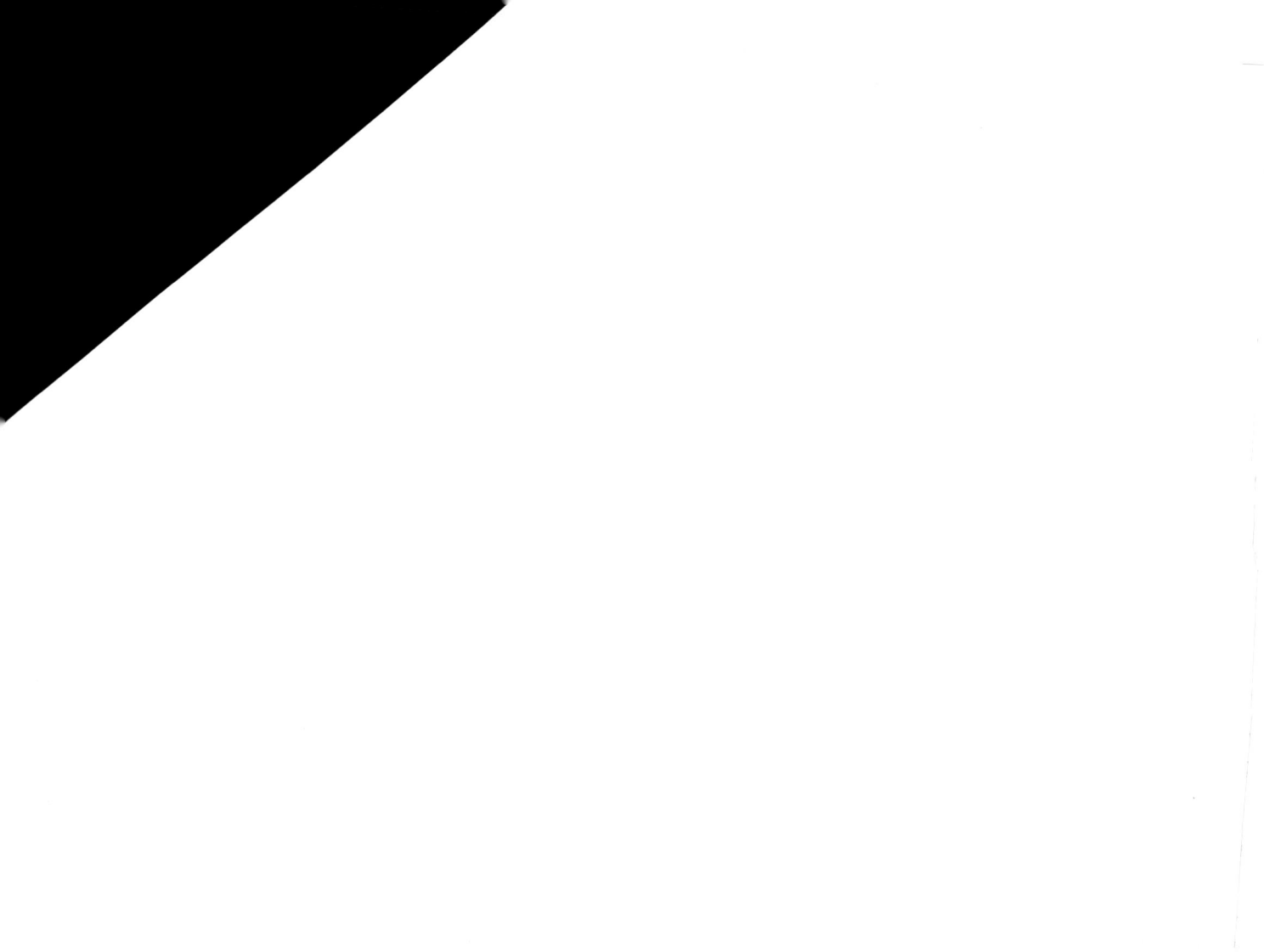

Dinky Toys

'much loved' Dinky Toys of the 1950s

Kim Sayer

dewi lewis publishing

Dinky Toys

I have fond memories of my Dinky toys and, like most boys of my generation, I had quite a fleet. There was the big Blaw-Knox bulldozer that Father Christmas brought when I was six. Rushing along the corridor at some ungodly hour to show it to my parents, I fell over. It received its first chip and I received a nasty cut from the driver's head. Various cars come to mind, particularly racing cars as these were in reach of saved pocket money. I remember the silver Napier-Railton Special, as driven by John Cobb, given to me as a reward for allowing my grandfather to pull out a loose tooth with a pair of pliers. Then there were some lorries, including a Foden eight-wheel tanker in two-tone blue and a smart maroon British Railways horsebox, the latter uniquely among my Dinkies lingering on in a cupboard well into adulthood. Indeed, it finally went only a few years ago. Some pre-war models, and a few planes, came from similar clear-outs by uncles and family friends, or from school swaps. I had a toy farm and so there was a green Field Marshall tractor. From the age of seven we had holidays in France and so I discovered French Dinkies. Soon I had a black Maigret-style Citroen Light Fifteen, exactly like the one my father drove. When he progressed to the stylish DS19, I had one too.

Dinky toys are memories and that is why this book is such a treat. For several decades the products of Frank Hornby's factories in Liverpool and elsewhere were an essential component of childhood and children from the 1930s to the 1980s and beyond were thrilled by that extraordinary and ever-changing range of models and colours. Like most children I played with my Dinkies and they had a hard life, at home, at school and in the garden. They were chipped and bashed and some were even repainted. Somehow that pristine newness never lasted and of course I threw away the box, immediately.

Years of duty as an expert in the miscellaneous department on BBC's *Antiques Roadshow* have taught me the error of my ways. I cannot count the number of times I have used that familiar phrase, 'Have you got the box?' I have seen thousands of Dinkies, including a few rarities worth hundreds of pounds. However, the majority have been chipped and bashed, just like mine, and therefore worth little in collecting terms. I have been shown immaculate Dinkies, mint in their box, by men of my age who had kept them that way since they were new. Fifty years on they can realise a tidy sum, but I cannot imagine a childhood filled with toys never played with. I remember one particular gentleman who, as a child, had saved his pocket money and bought two of everything, one to play with and one to put away for the future.

There are many books about Dinky toys and Dinky collecting, including price guides, and so the serious collector is well served. These are full of pictures of immaculate toys, posed carefully on their perfect boxes, designed to whet the appetite of the grown up and rather wealthy enthusiast. At its extreme, like so many of the other, newer collecting fields, an enthusiasm for Dinkies has echoes of the anorak, and little to do with the real world. For those of us who played with their toys, this is a refined and inaccessible world, driven by arcane and mysterious principles: model 135, the Triumph 2000, was made between 1963 and 1969, and in standard metallic green or blue it is worth up to £50 but in British racing green the value is up to £1000.

This book is different. It is full of photographs of the toys we loved, in the state that we knew them, that is to say chipped and bashed. It is, as a result, a real vision of a real childhood. Every photograph tells a story and they are witty, entertaining and full of memories, an enduring nostalgia trip for those of us who actually enjoyed playing with our Dinky toys.

Paul Atterbury

*This popular Trojan Van is supplied with the name
'OXO' in characteristic style on each side.*

Trojan 15cwt 'OXO' Van, 1953-54.

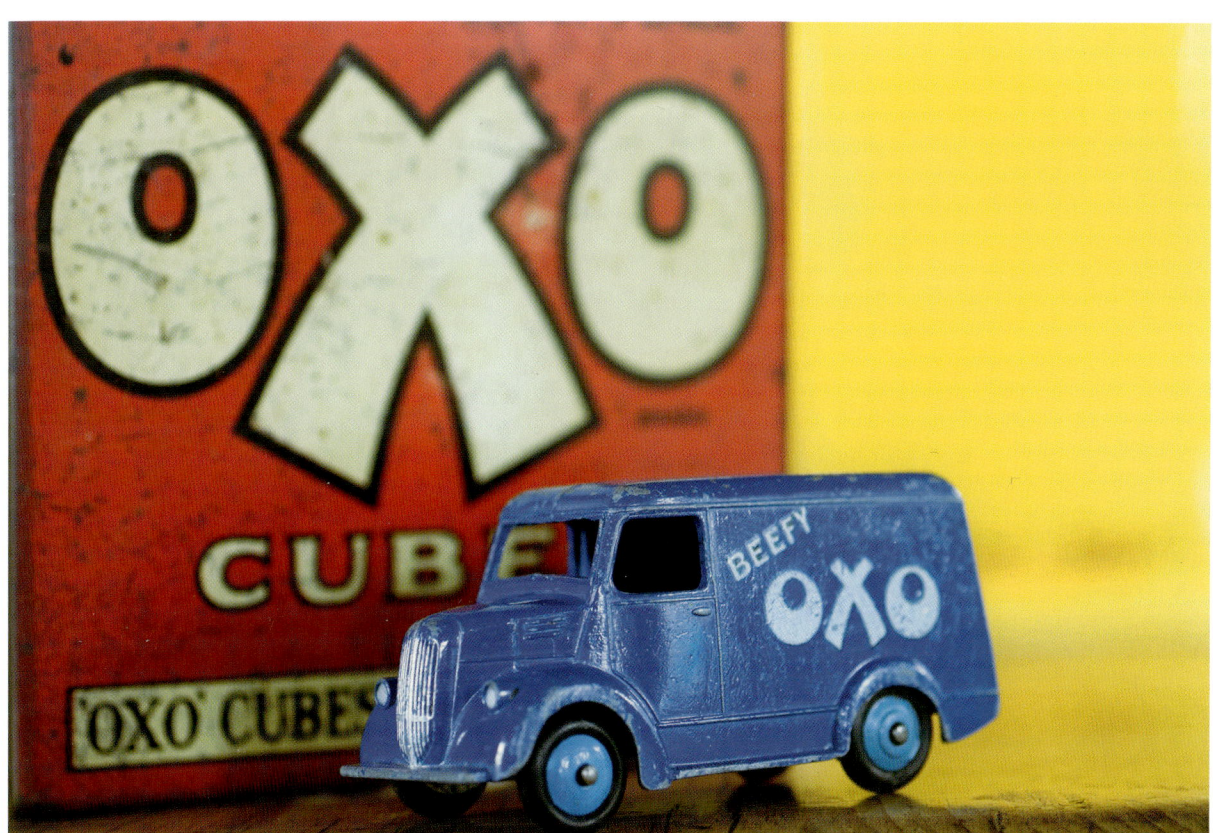

In its new finish of green, with apple symbol and the name 'CYDRAX' on the sides, the Trojan Van assumes a new character and becomes another attractive model for enthusiastic collectors.

Trojan 15cwt 'CYDRAX' Van, 1957-59.

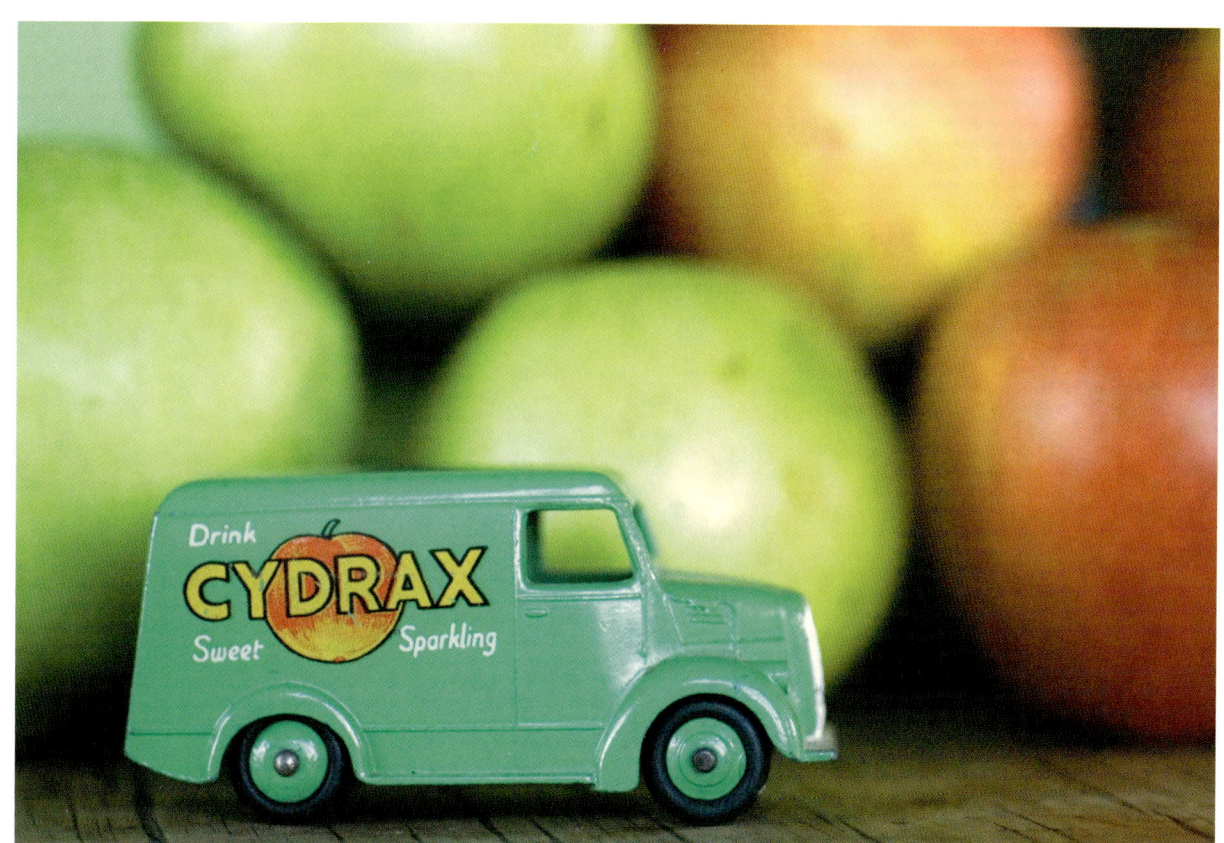

This version of the popular 10cwt van is now available in the attractive 'OVALTINE' finish.

Bedford 10cwt 'OVALTINE' Van, 1955-60.

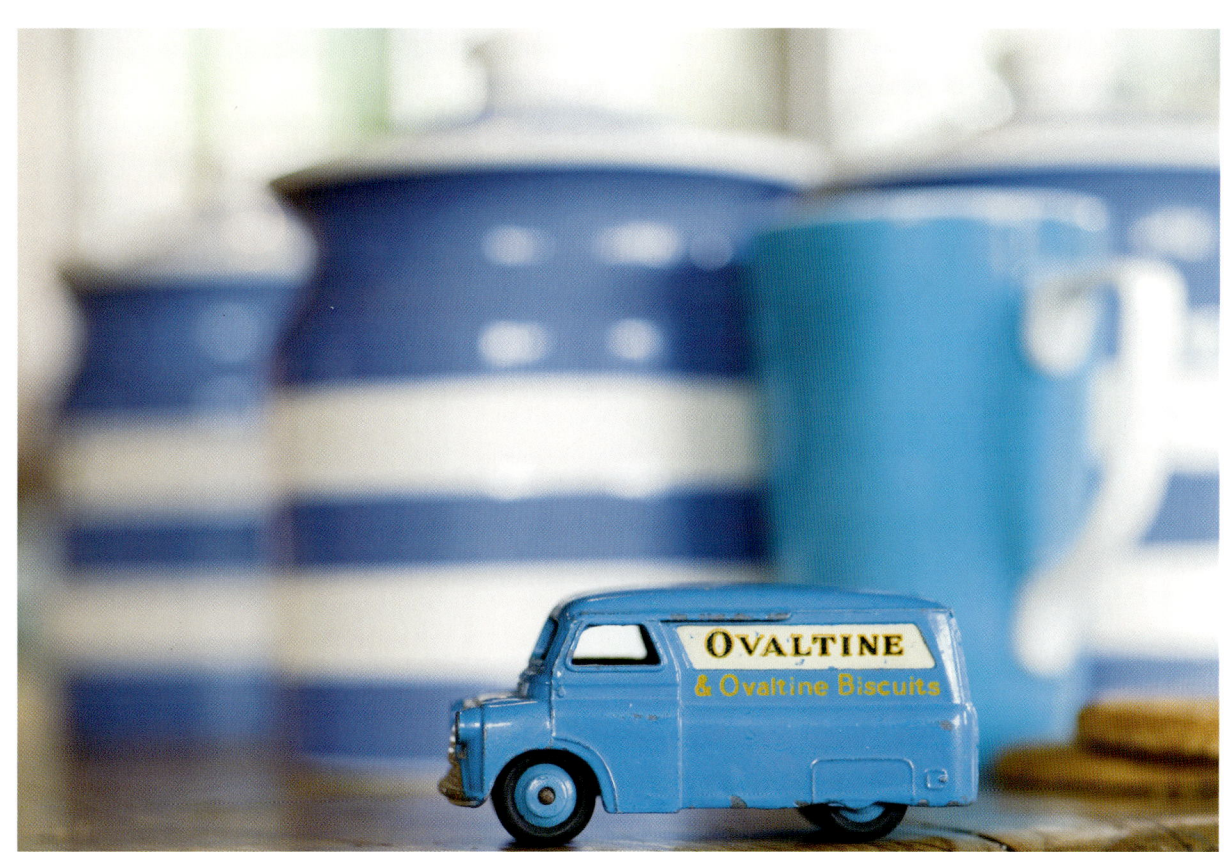

The distinctive character of the Austin A40 Van shows to advantage in this new colour finish of bright red with the name 'NESTLÉ'S' in gold on both side panels.

Austin A40 'NESTLÉ'S' Van, 1955-63.

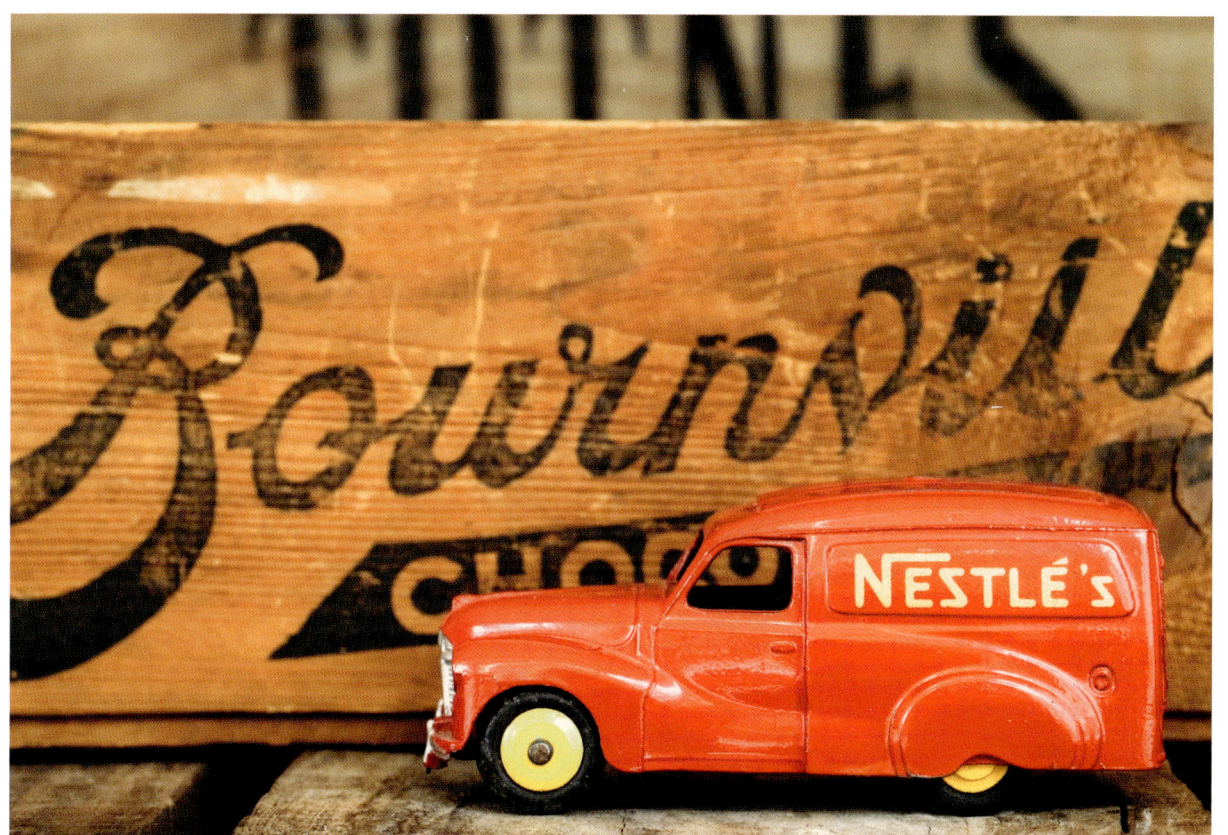

This well known Morris 10cwt Van is a splendid addition to the Dinky Toys range with 'CAPSTAN' cigarettes neatly reproduced on the sides.

Morris 10cwt 'CAPSTAN' Van, 1957-59.

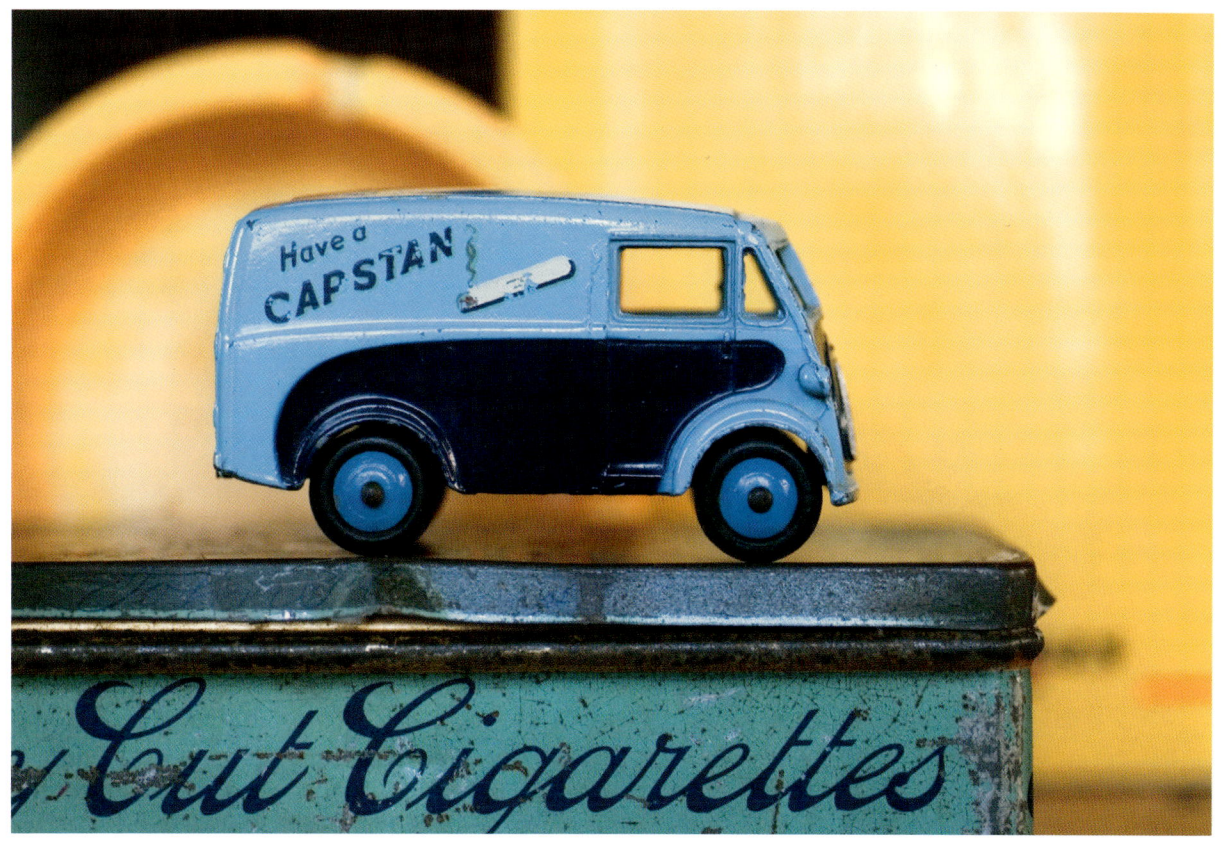

This popular delivery van, a familiar sight throughout the country, now has a Dinky Toys counterpart, finished in bright red with the name 'Brooke Bond Tea' in white on the sides.

Trojan 15cwt 'Brooke Bond Tea' Van, 1957-60.

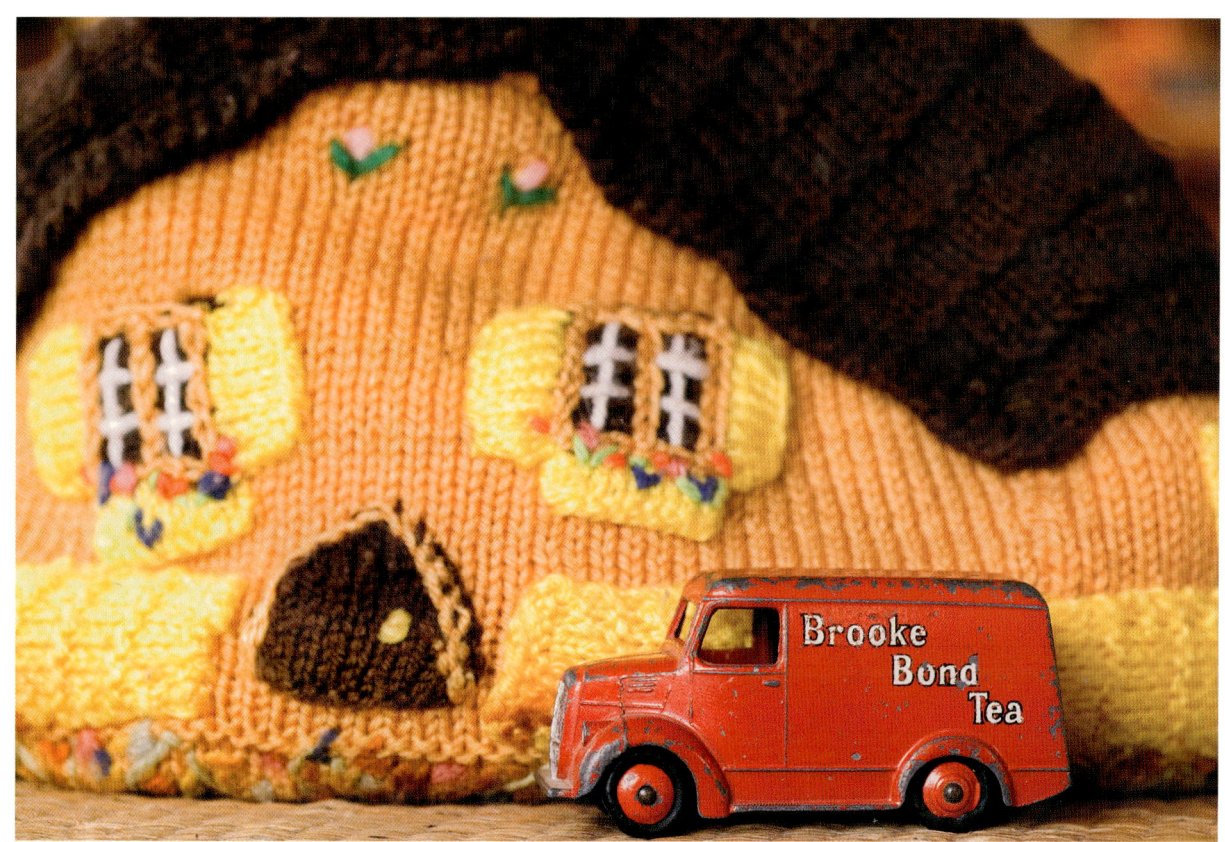

Loudspeaker Van, 1948-57.
Re-issue of pre-war 28 van series.

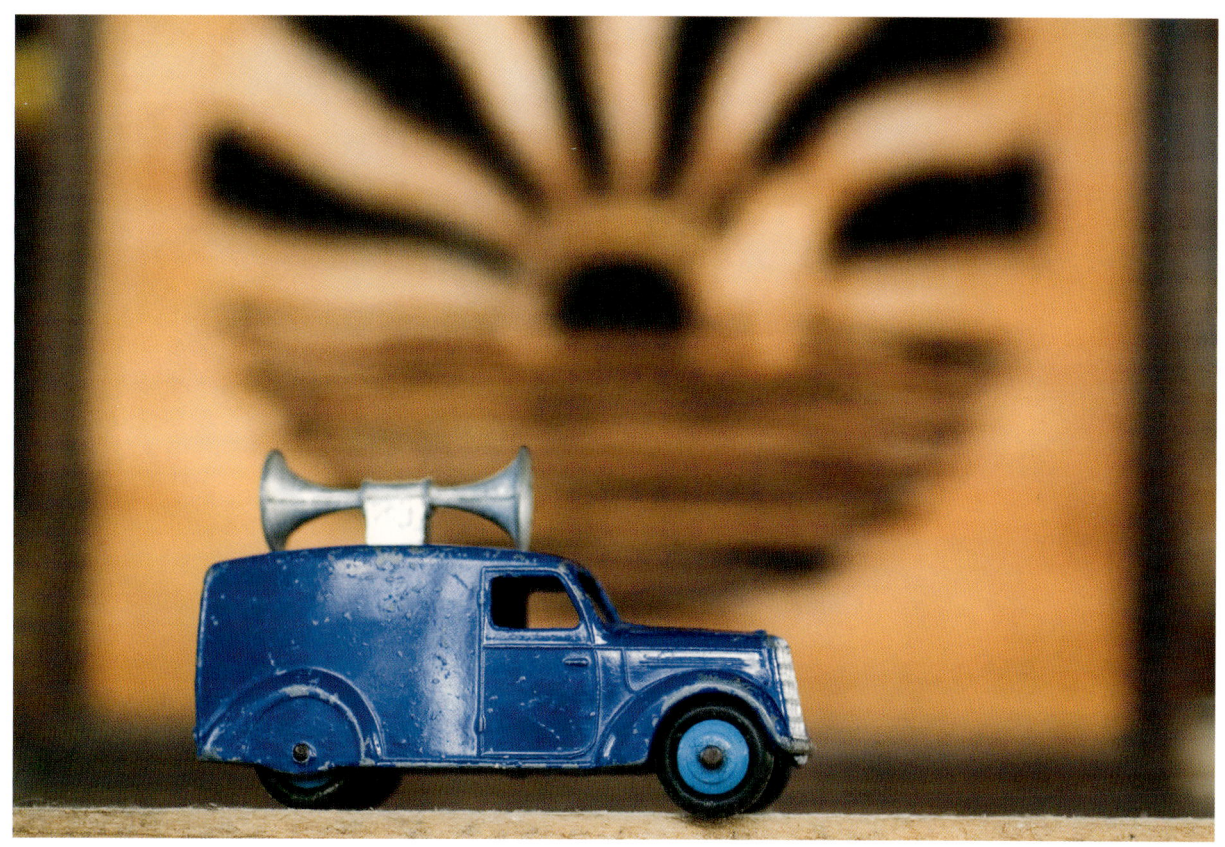

Peugeot 'Postes' Van, 1954-59.
Made in France.

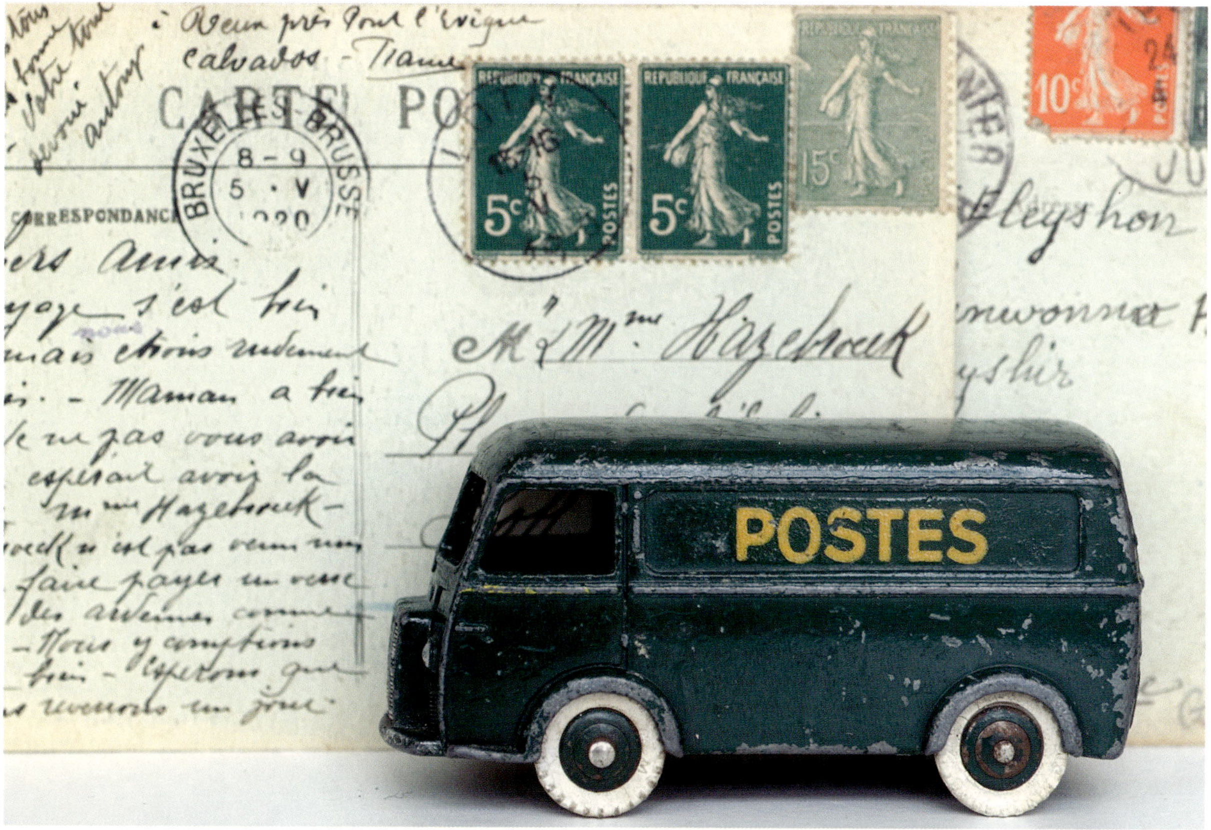
REPUBLIQUE FRANÇAISE
5c
POSTES
15c
10c
POSTES

In regulation green finish, with lettering and Royal Crown on both sides, here is an exact miniature of a Morris Van used in large numbers as a service vehicle, fitted with ladder on roof.

Morris Telephone Service Van, 1956-61.

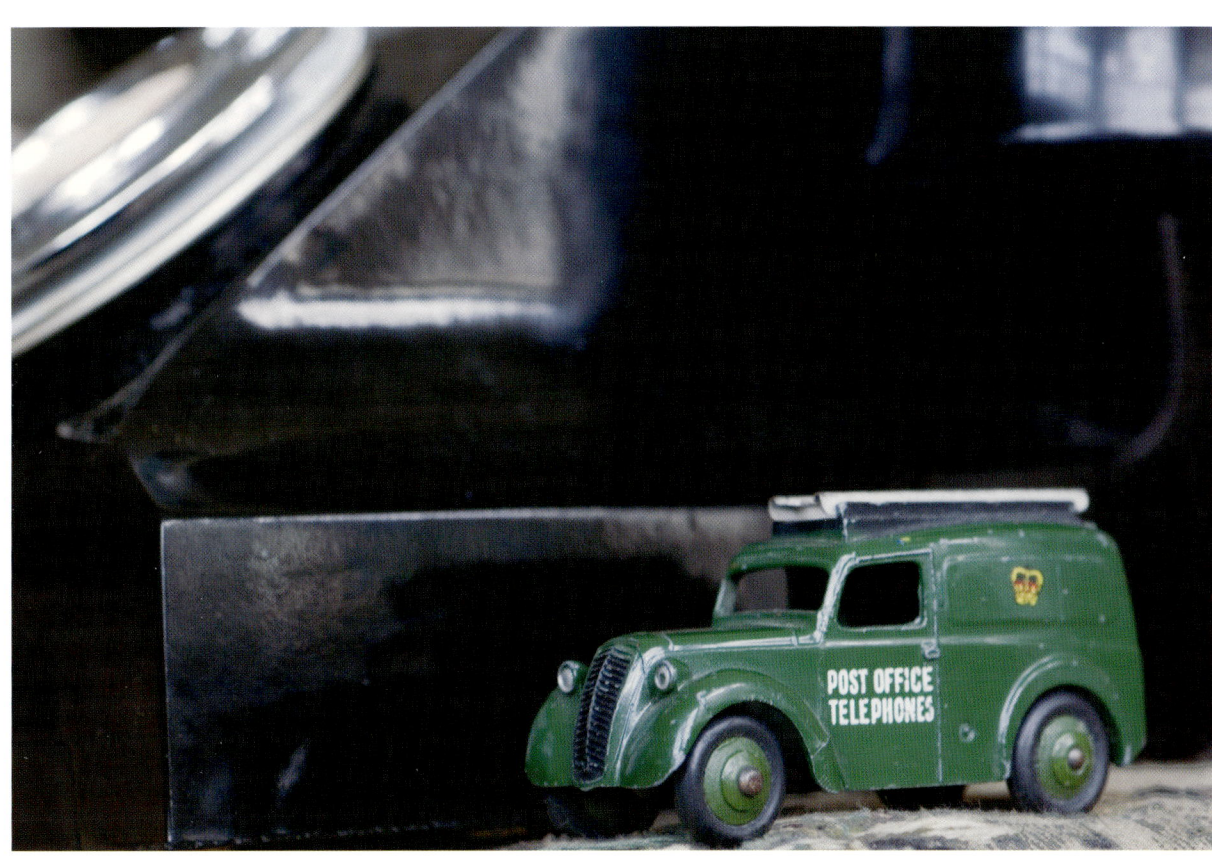

A realistic reproduction of a modern style tanker.

Petrol Tanker Wagon 'Petrol', 1946-50.
Re-issue of pre-war 25 model.

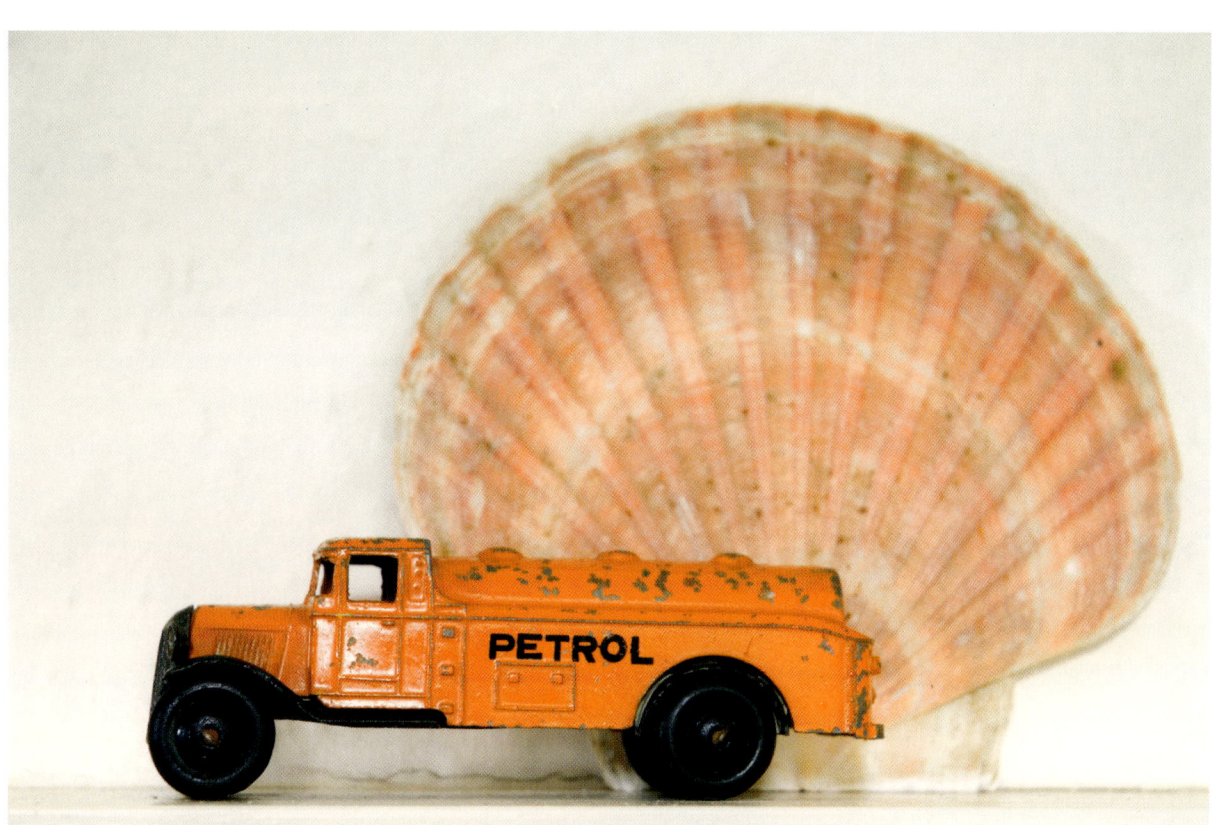

Petrol Tanker Studebaker, 'National Benzole Mixture', 1957-59.
Foden 14-Ton Tanker 'Regent', 1955-57.
Austin A40 Van 'Shell-BP', 1954-65.
Trojan 15cwt Van 'Esso', 1951-57.

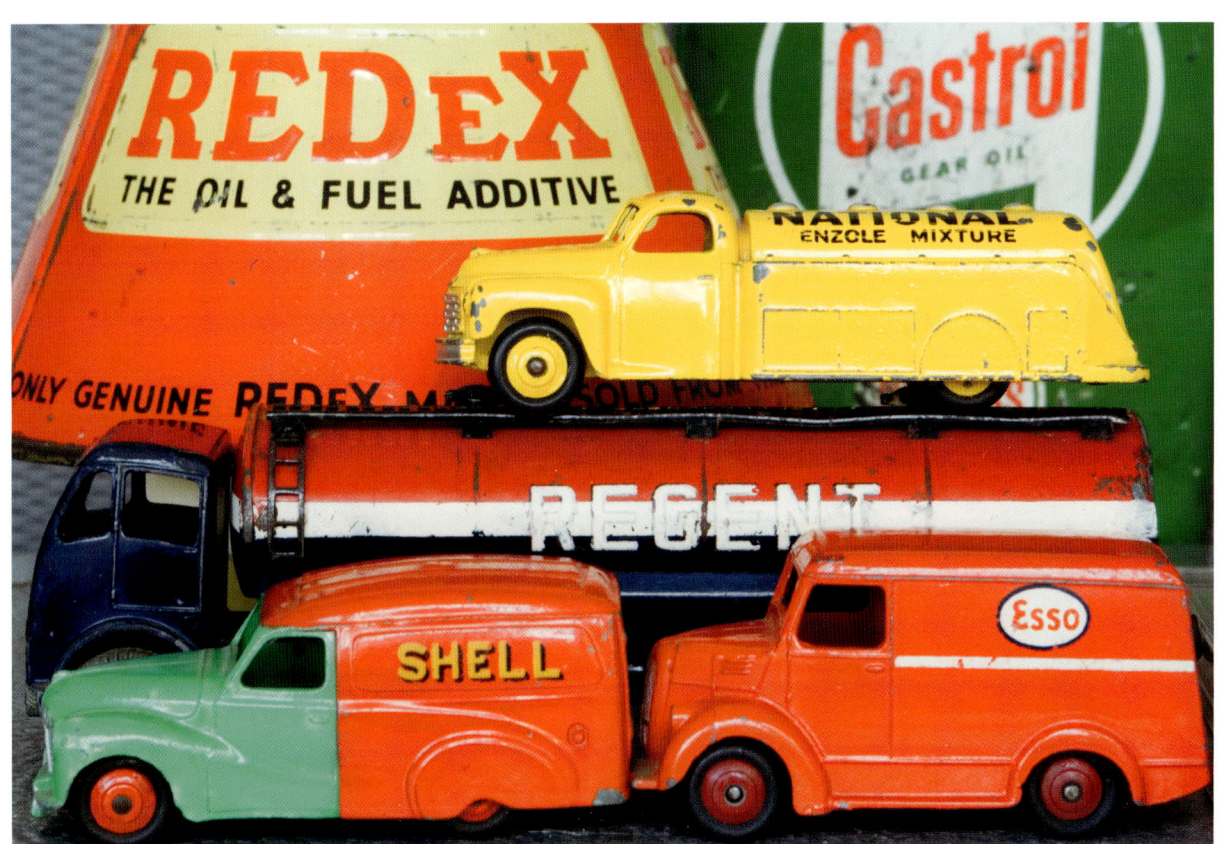

A fine model of one of the giant tankers familiar on our roads.

Dinky Supertoy Foden 14-Ton Tanker, 1948-53.

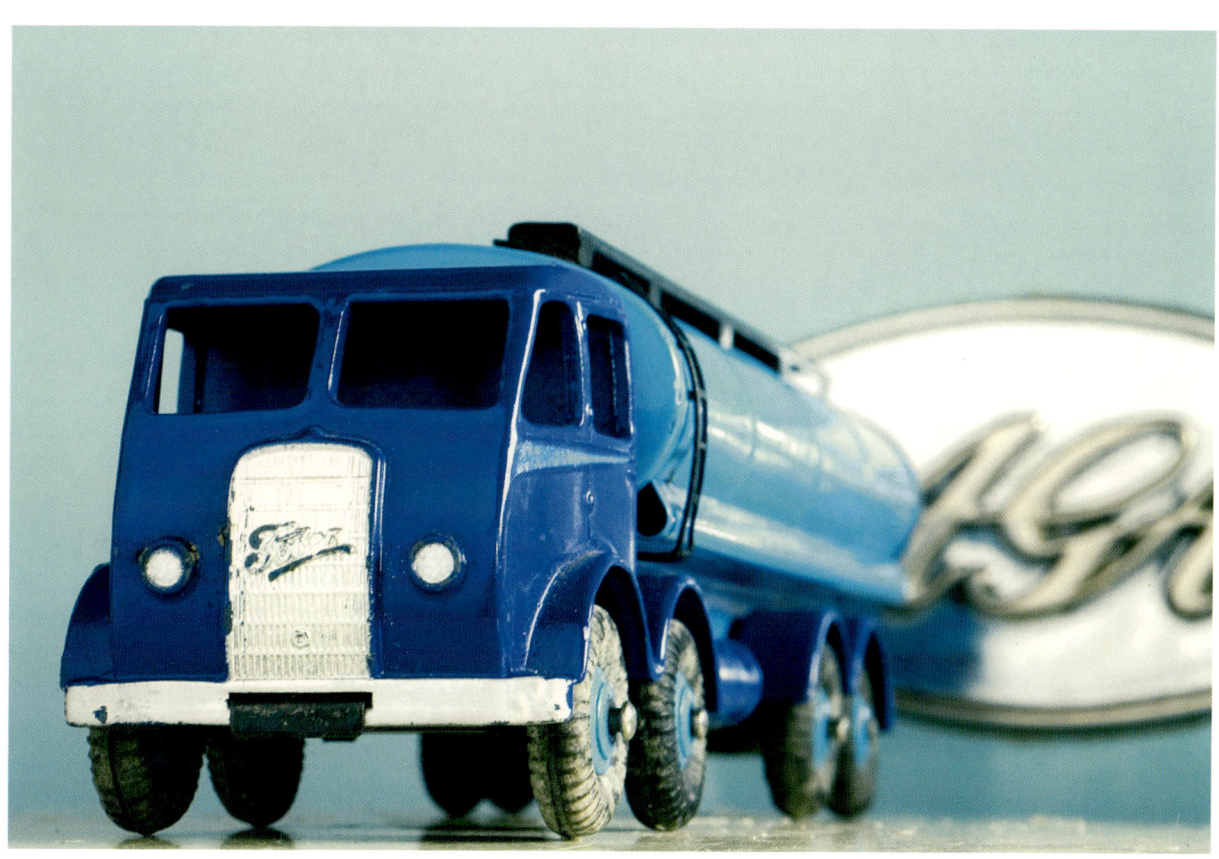

Large capacity van body with opening double doors at rear.

Guy Van 'Slumberland', 1949-51.

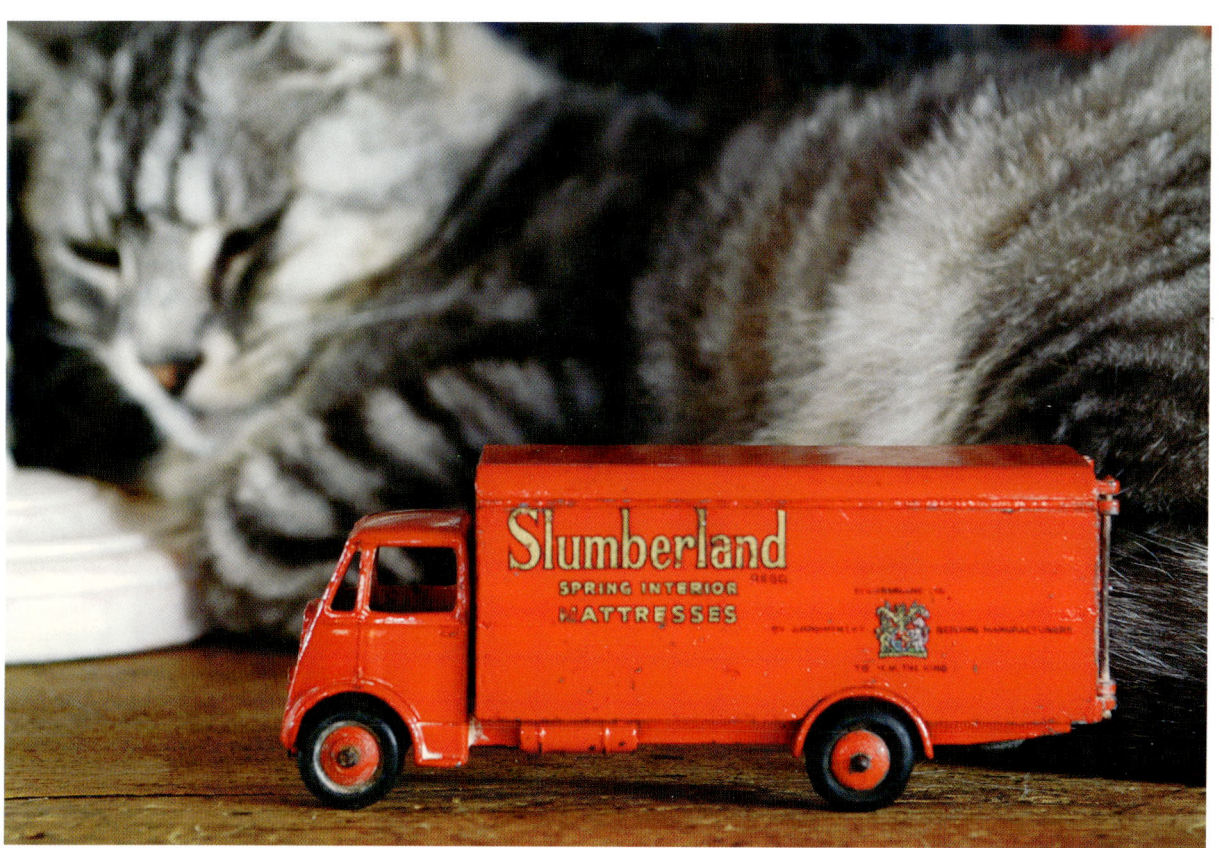

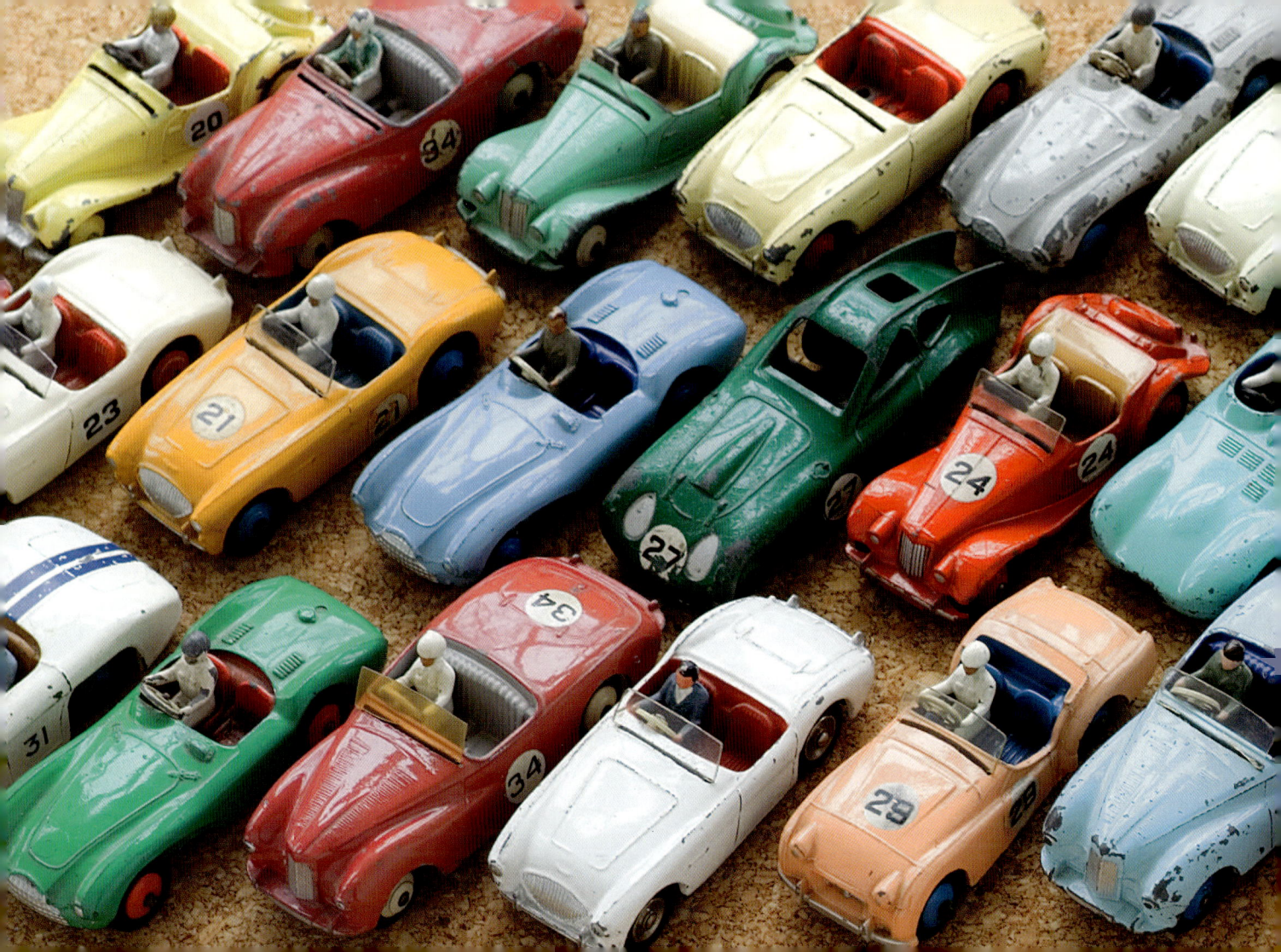

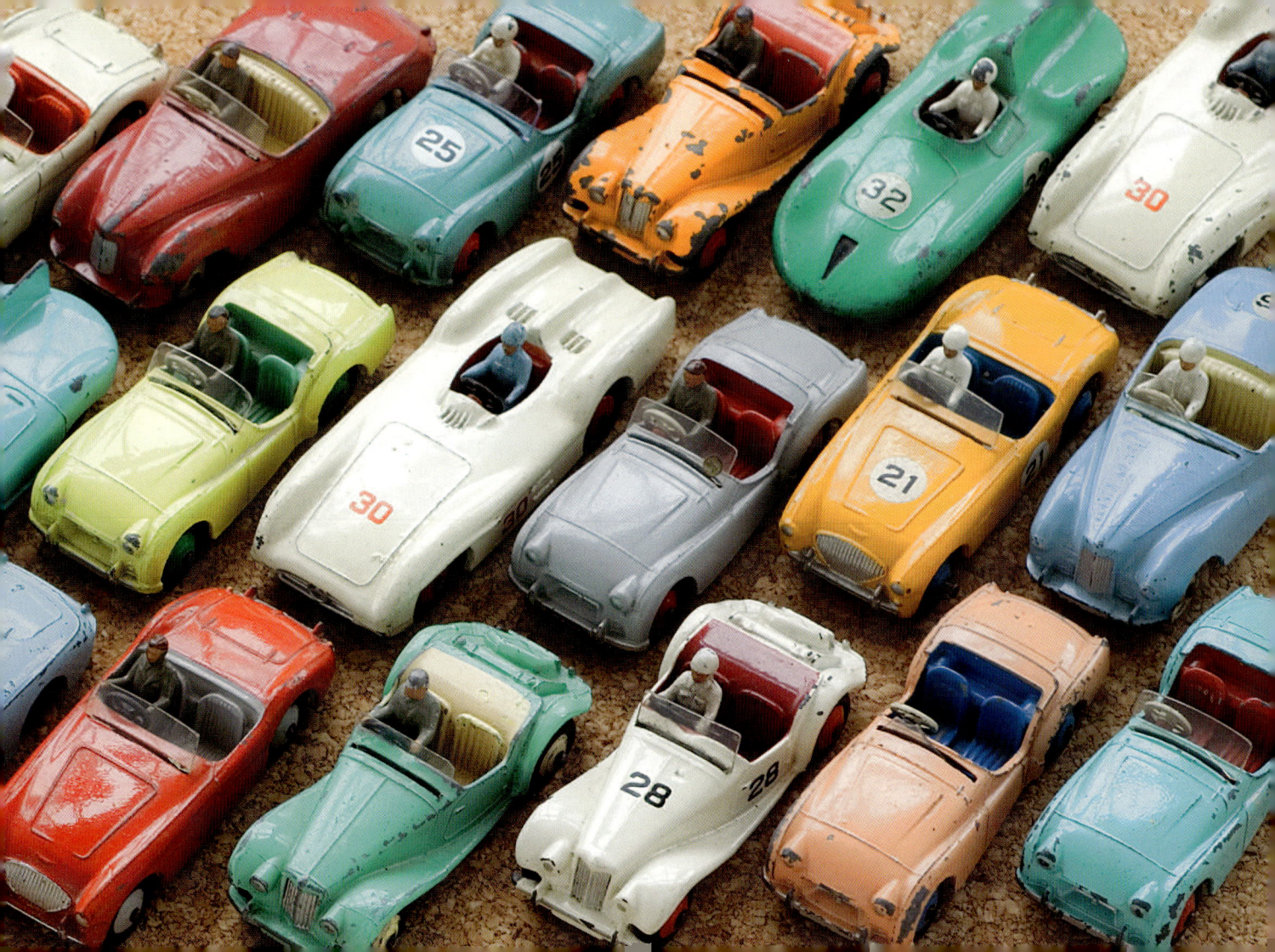

A scale model of one of the finest equipped sports cars on the road.

Sunbeam Talbot Sports, 1940-54.

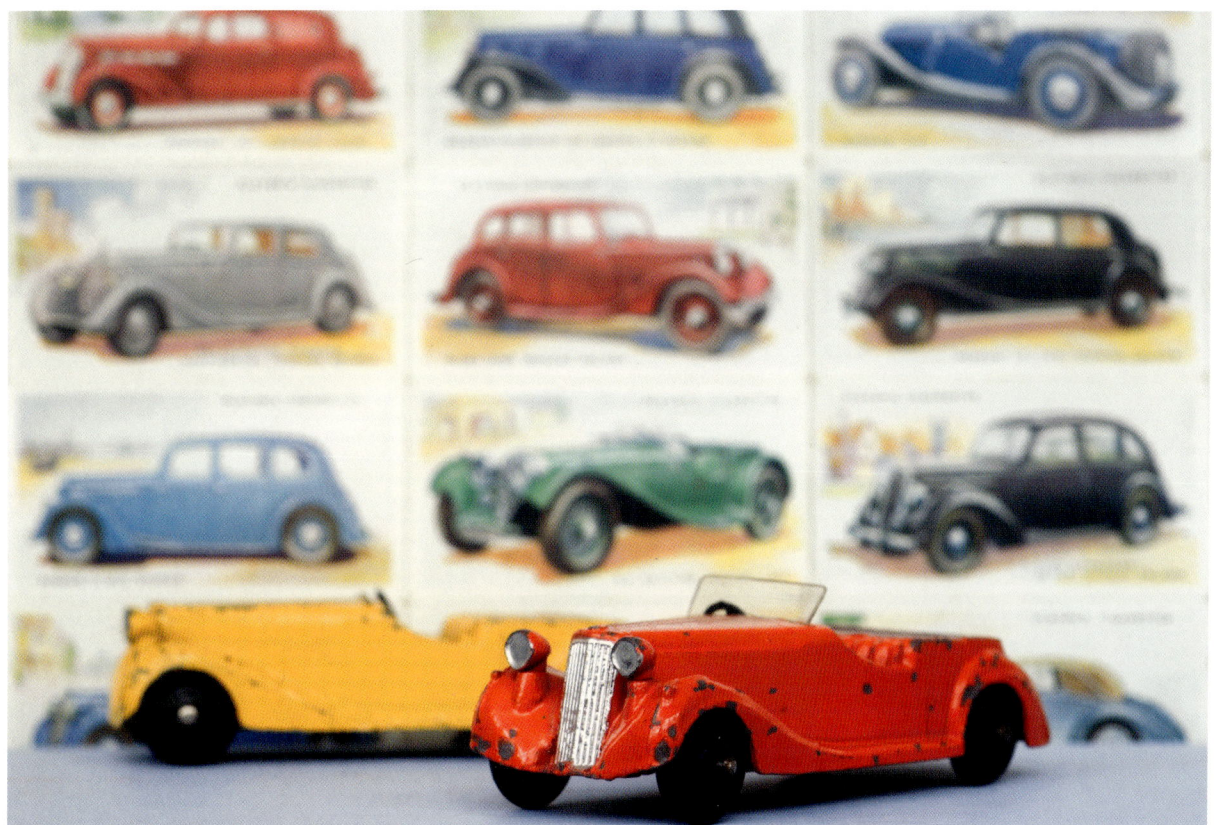

This famous fixed-head two seater is a leader in its class. Its graceful lines are faithfully reproduced in this model.

Jaguar XK120 Coupe, 1954-62.

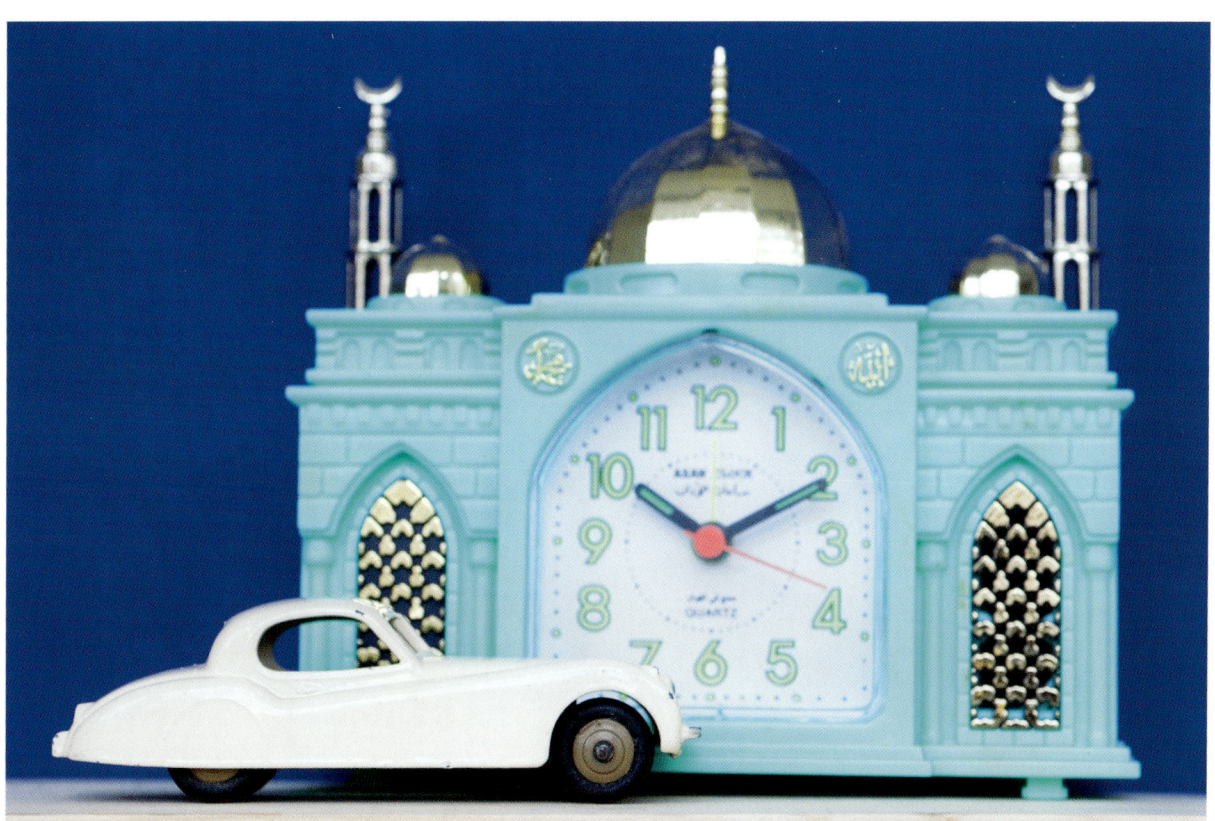

Here are superb reproductions of popular British high-performance two seater sports cars. Fitted with windscreens and drivers in white racing kit, with competition number discs on sides and bonnets.

Sunbeam Alpine, 1955-59 (back). Austin Healey, 1955-59 (left). MG Midget, 1955-59 (centre). Triumph TR2, 1956-59 (right).

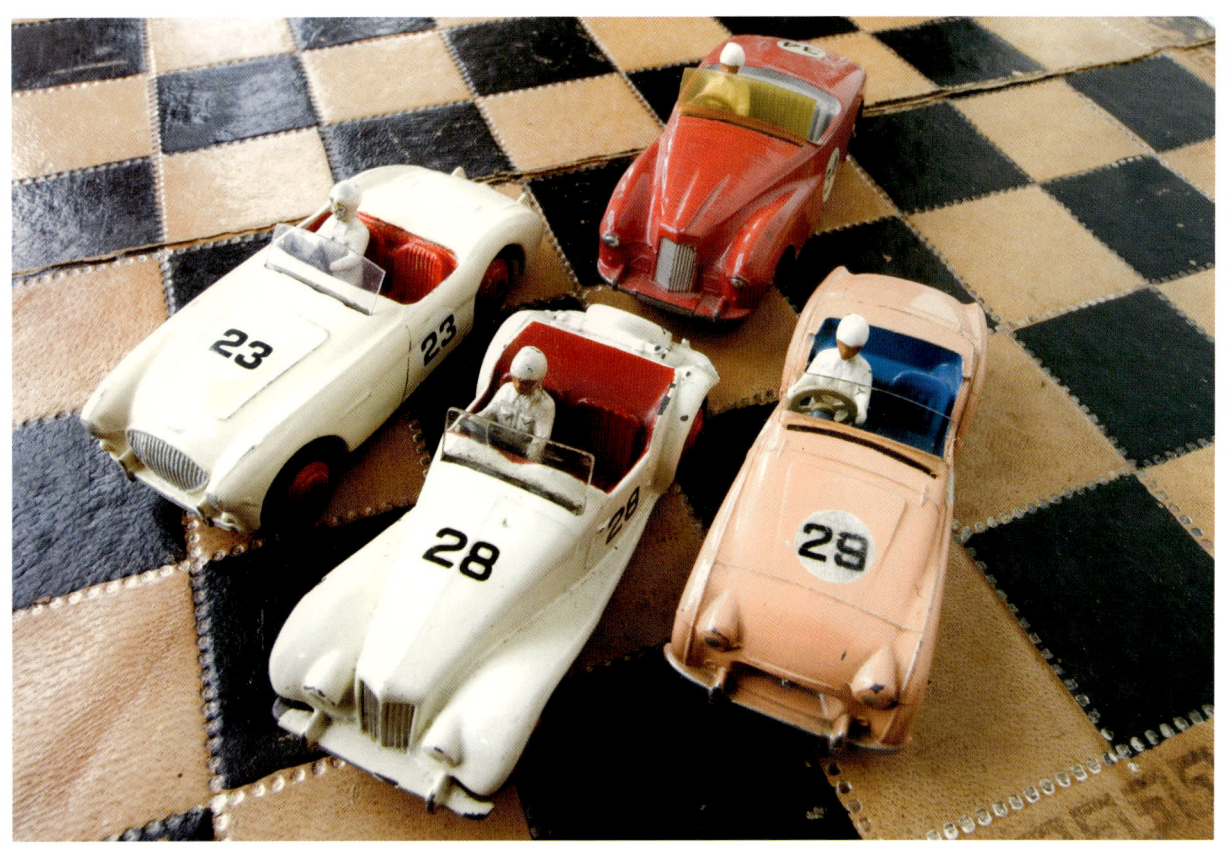

This popular British sports car is now available in touring finish with civilian driver. It is available in a choice of two colour schemes and makes a gay addition to any Dinky Toys collection.

Triumph TR2 (Touring Finish), 1957-62.

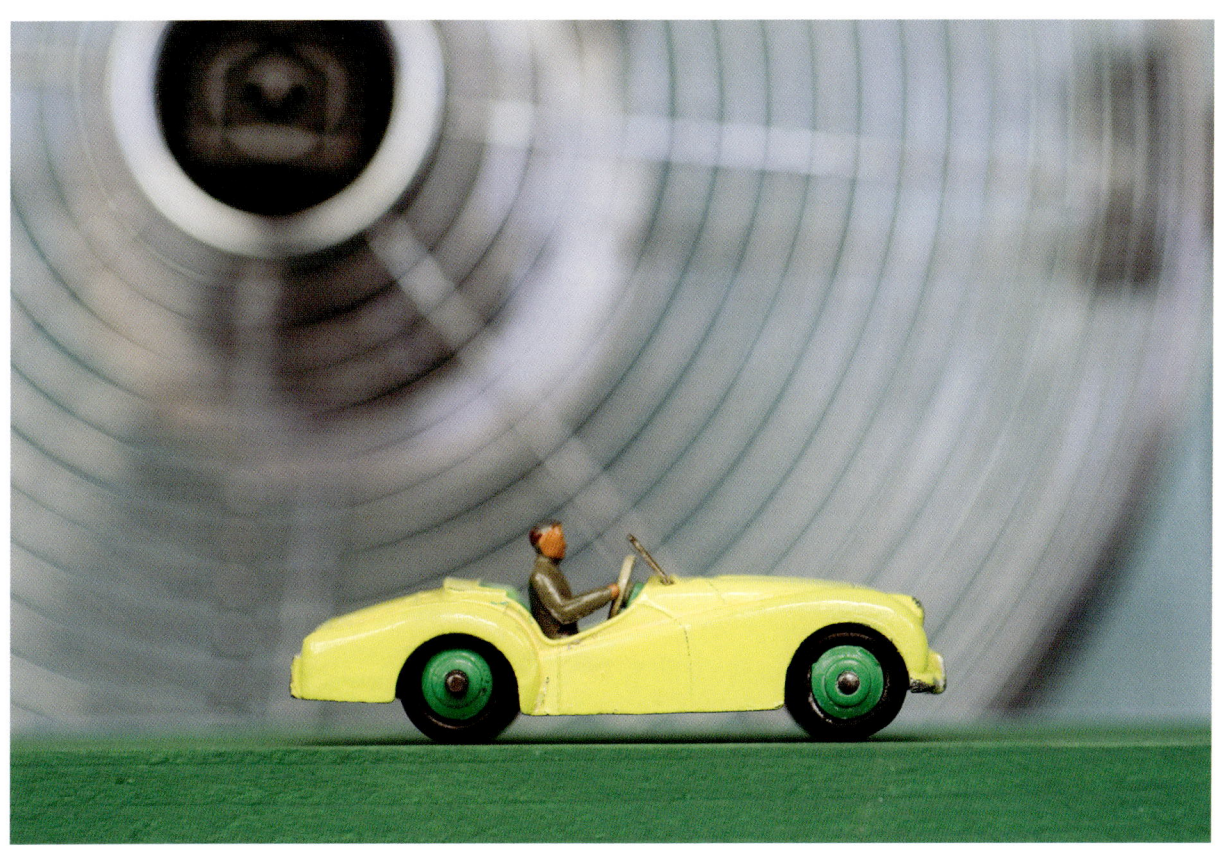

This famous race-winner is an exciting addition to the Dinky Toys range.

Aston Martin (Touring Finish), 1957-60.

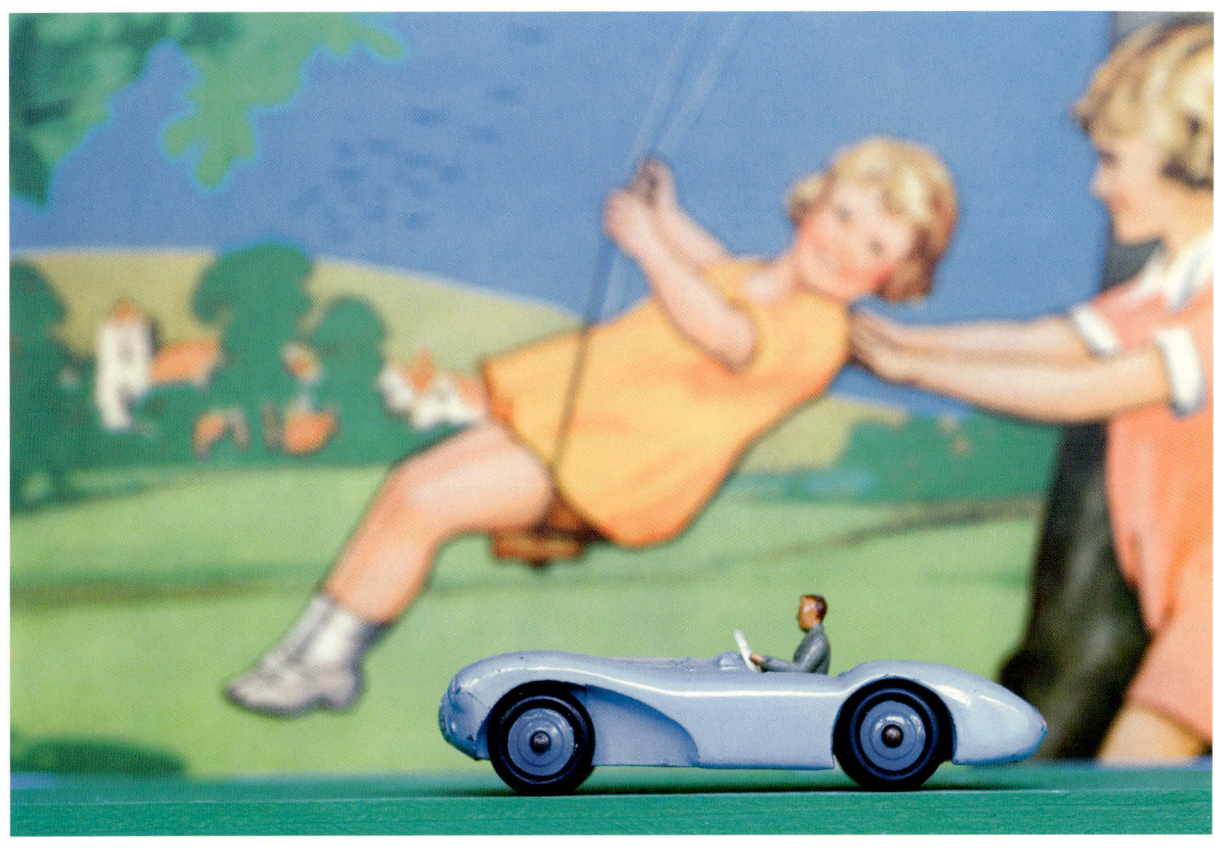

*Here is an appealing model of the TF series MG Midget,
the world's most popular sports car.*

MG Midget (Touring Finish), 1957-60.

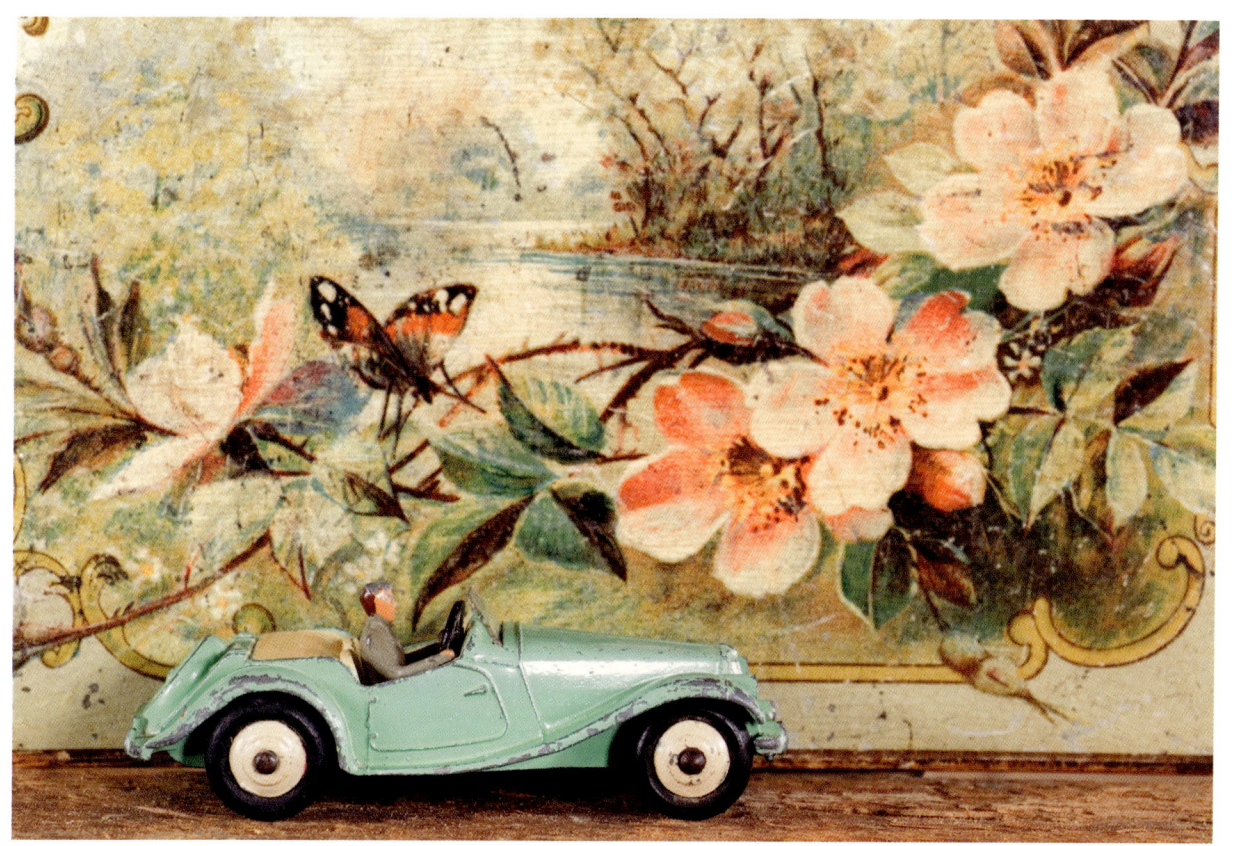

*This new masterpiece of the modeller's art is a perfect
miniature of one of today's most famous sports cars.*

Austin Healey (Touring Finish), 1957-60.

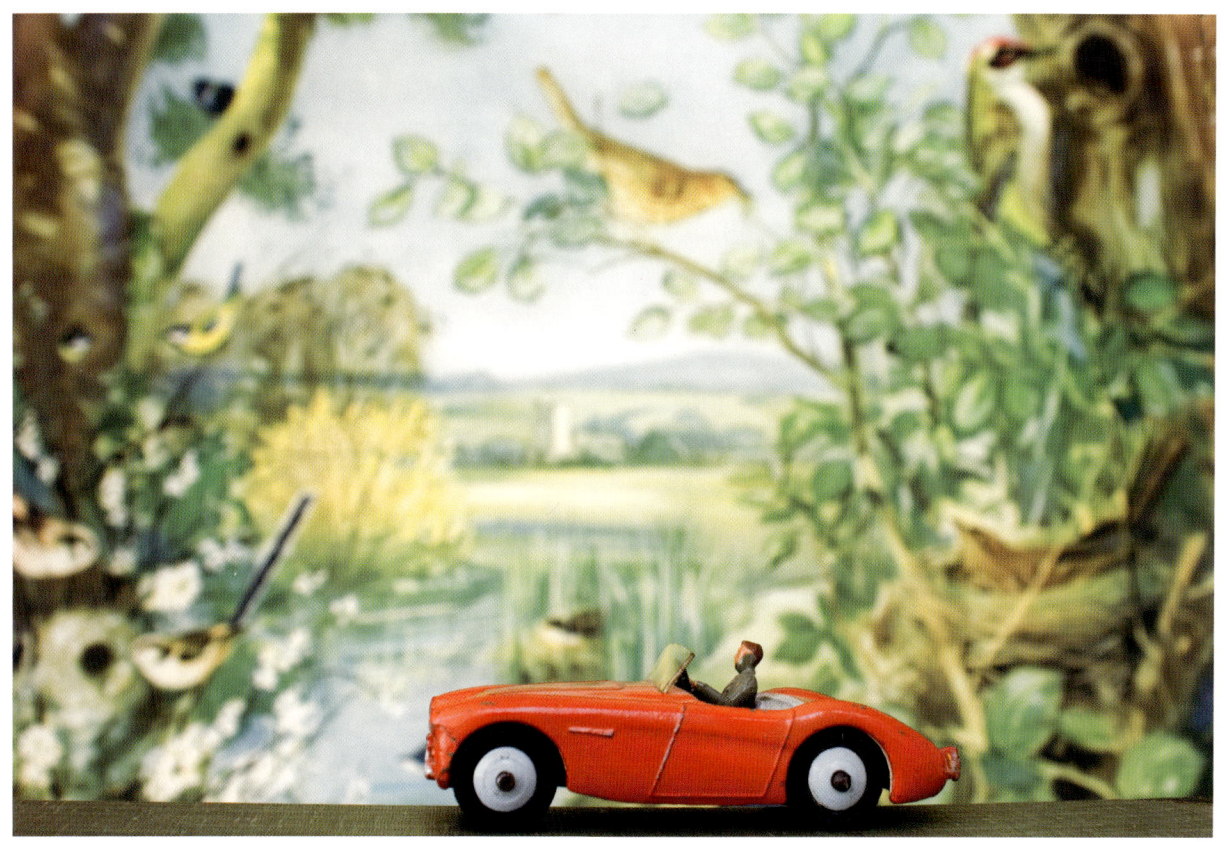

'Speed of The Wind' Racing Car, 1936-57.
Re-issue of pre-war 23e model.

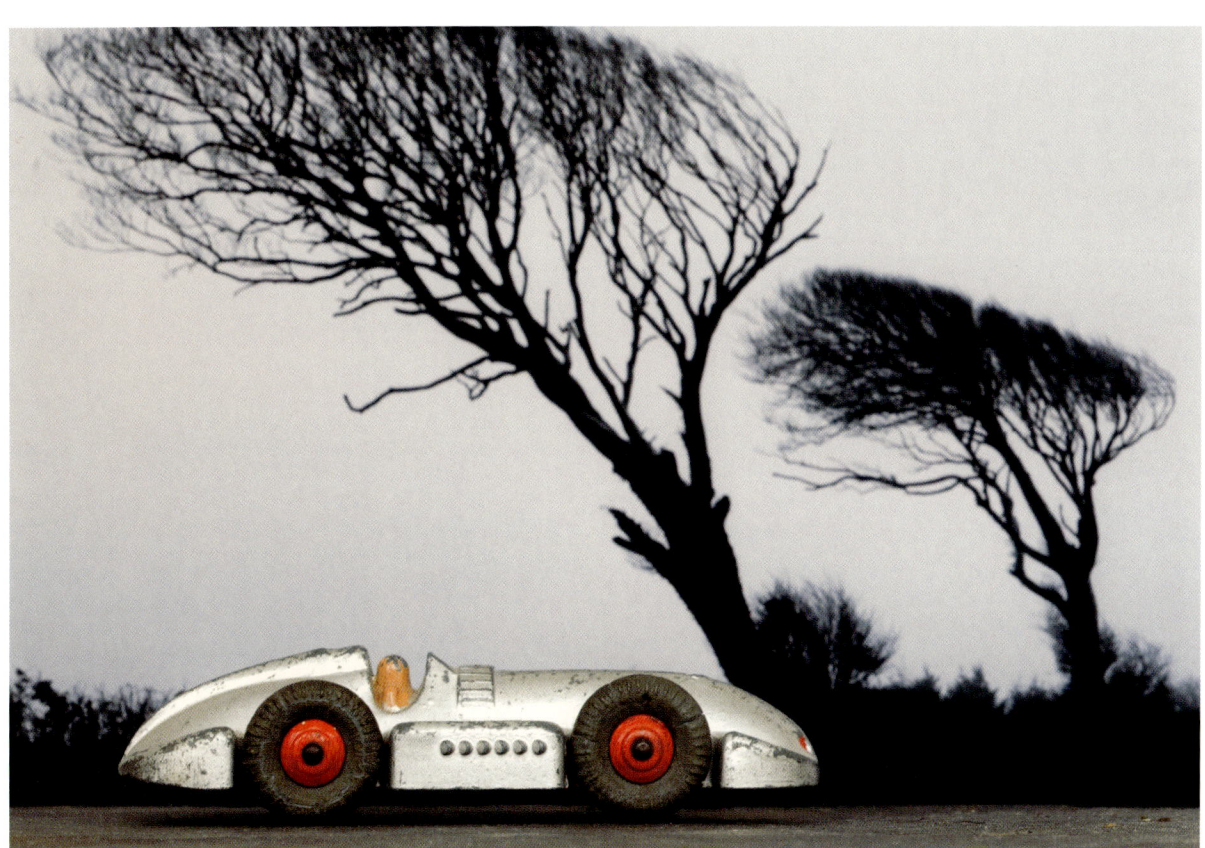

Racing Cars, 1934-56.
Re-issue of 23a model.

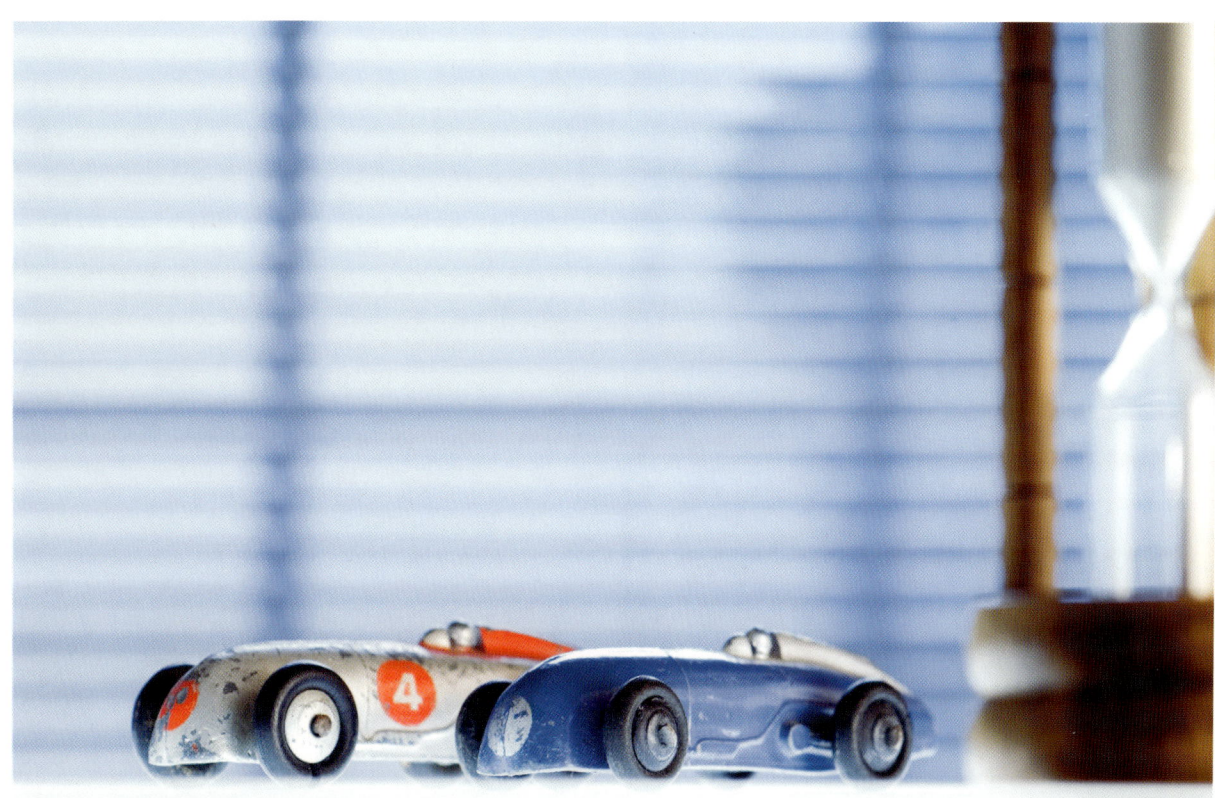

A scale miniature of the Italian built Maserati, which has earned a great reputation by its performances in international track events.

Maserati Racing Car, 1953-64.

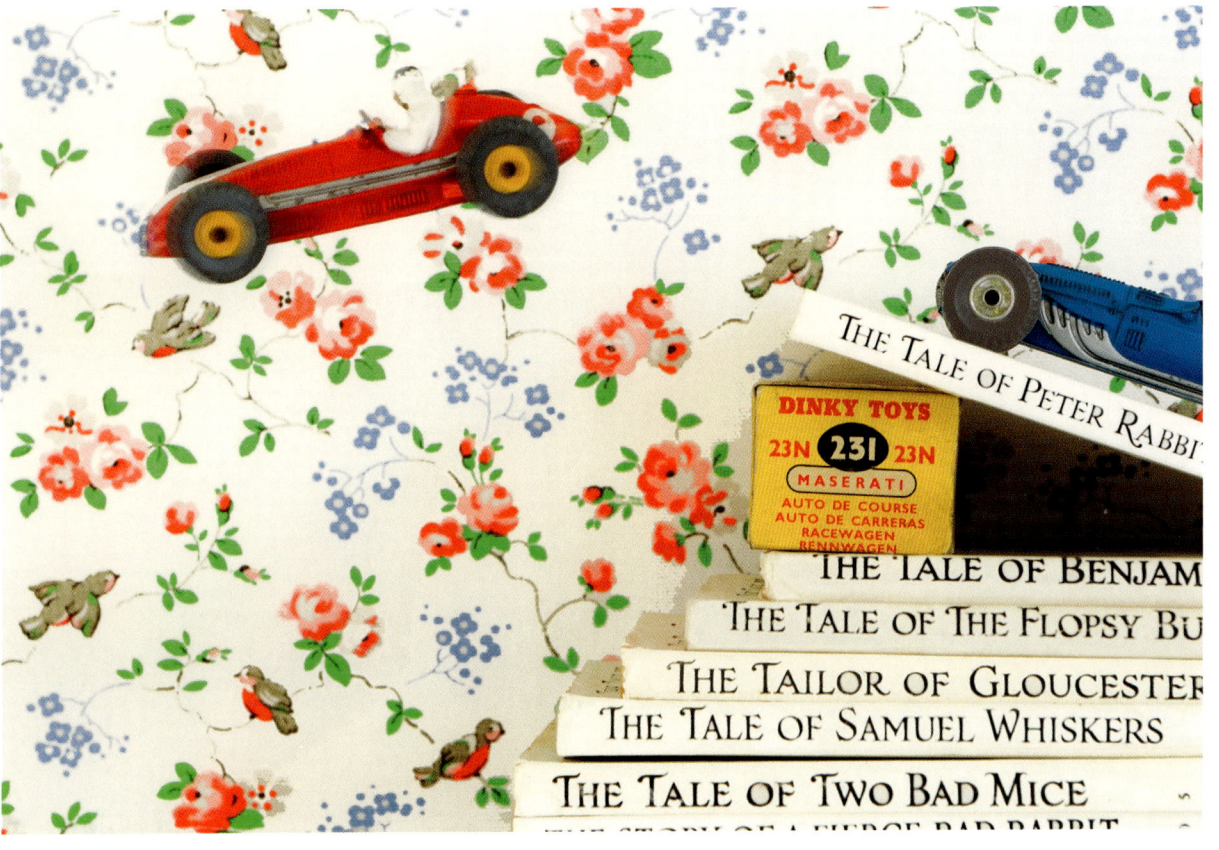

DINKY TOYS
23N **231** 23N
MASERATI
AUTO DE COURSE
AUTO DE CARRERAS
RACEWAGEN
RENNWAGEN

THE TALE OF PETER RABBIT

THE TALE OF BENJAM

THE TALE OF THE FLOPSY BU

THE TAILOR OF GLOUCESTER

THE TALE OF SAMUEL WHISKERS

THE TALE OF TWO BAD MICE

THE STORY OF A FIERCE BAD RABBIT

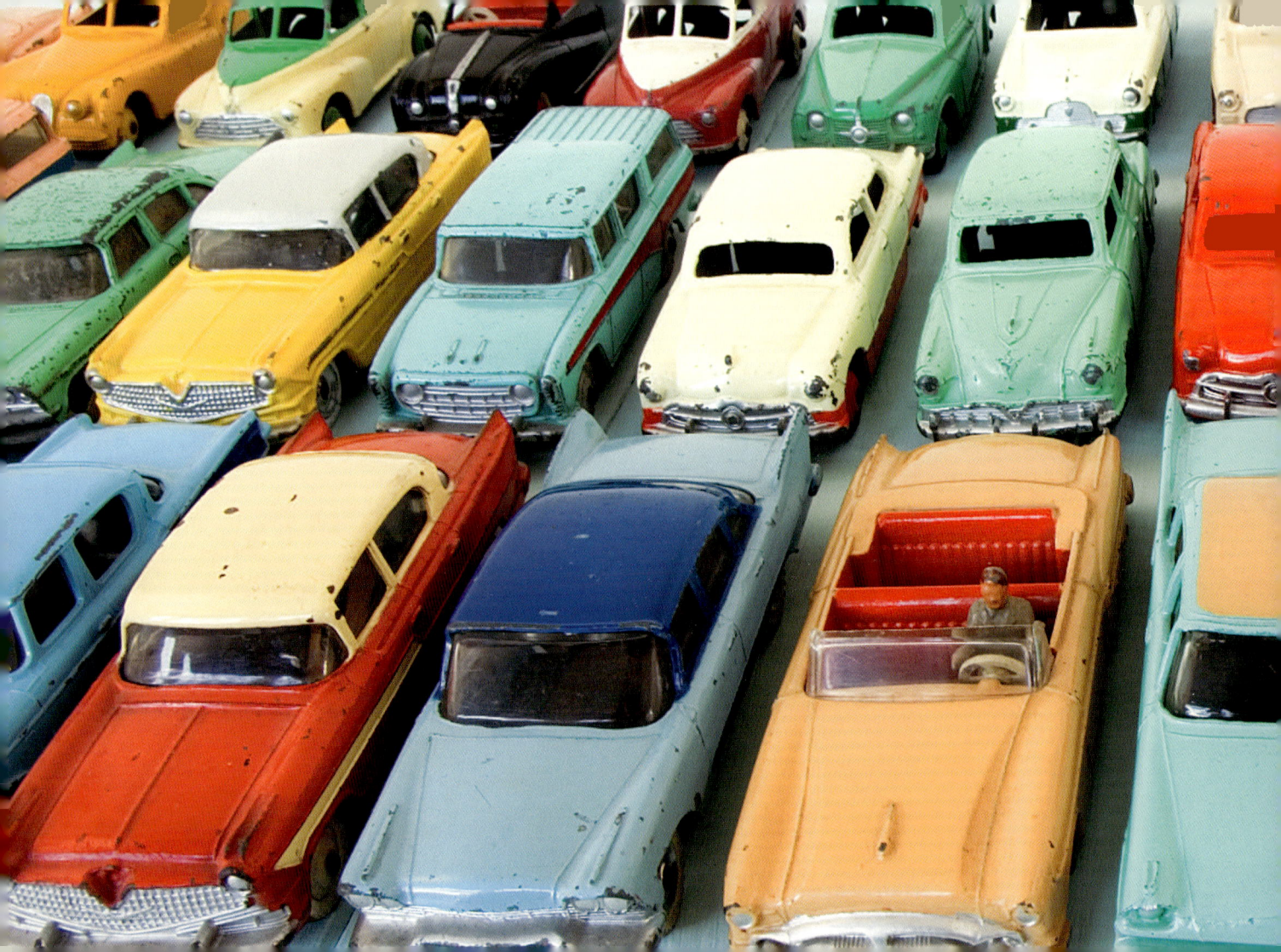

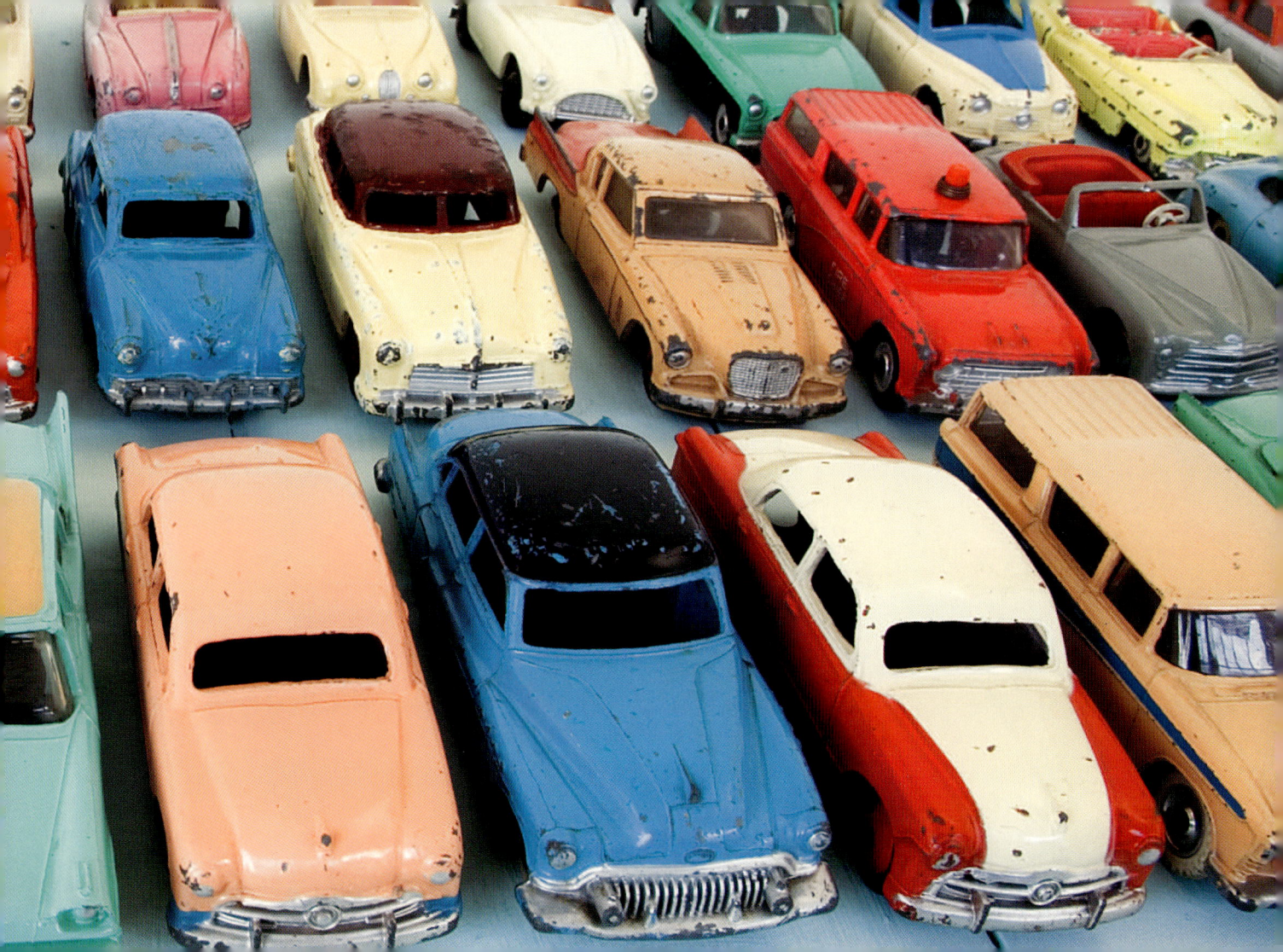

Rolls Royce, 1935-50.
Re-issue of pre-war 30 series.

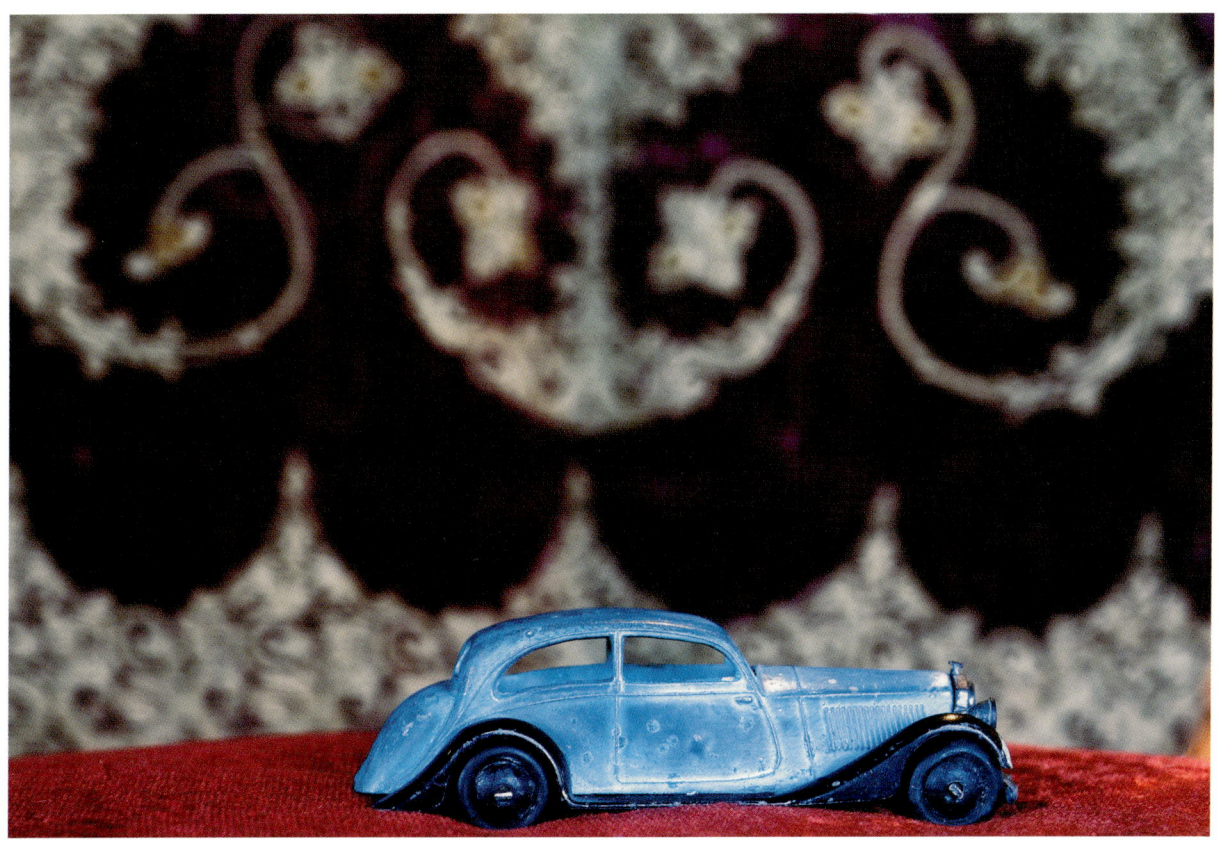

Daimler, 1935-50.
Re-issue of pre-war 30 series.

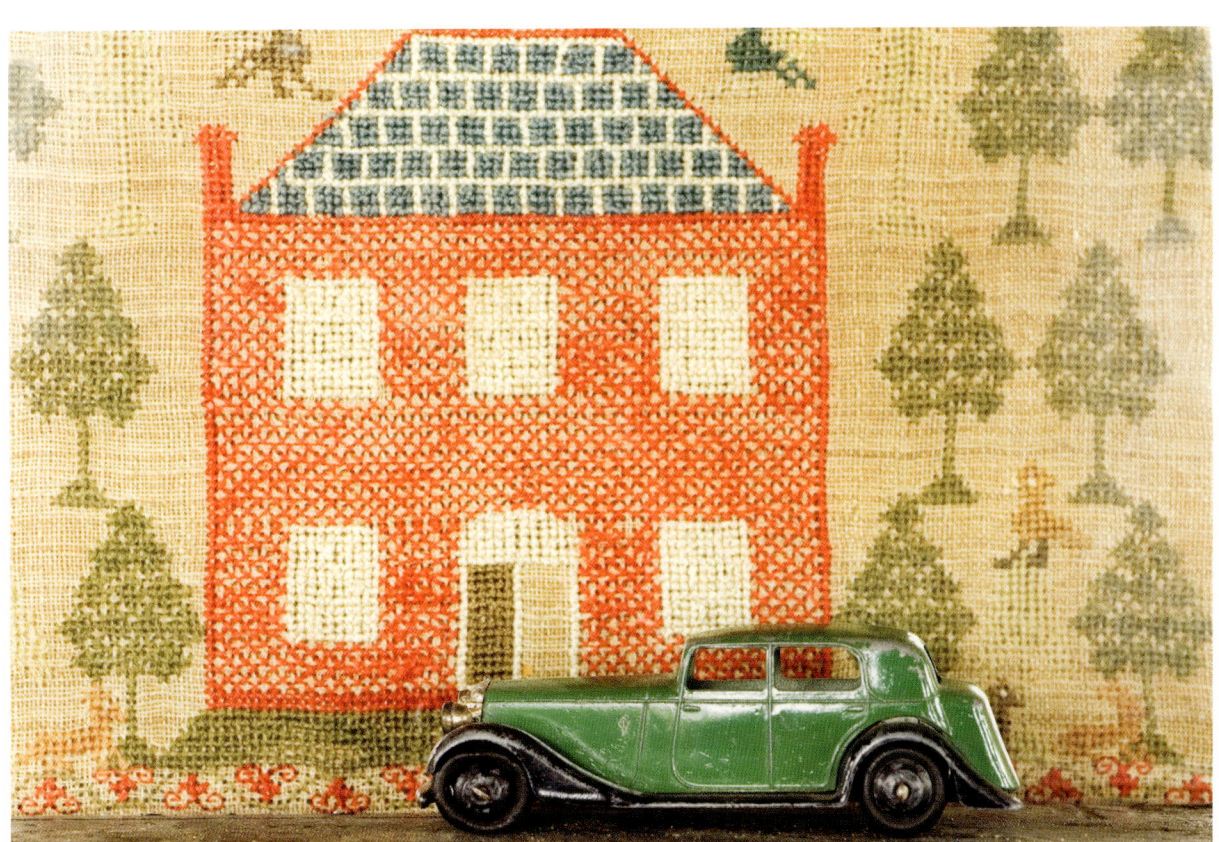

Reproduces perfectly the characteristic features of this famous car.

Riley Saloon, 1947-60.

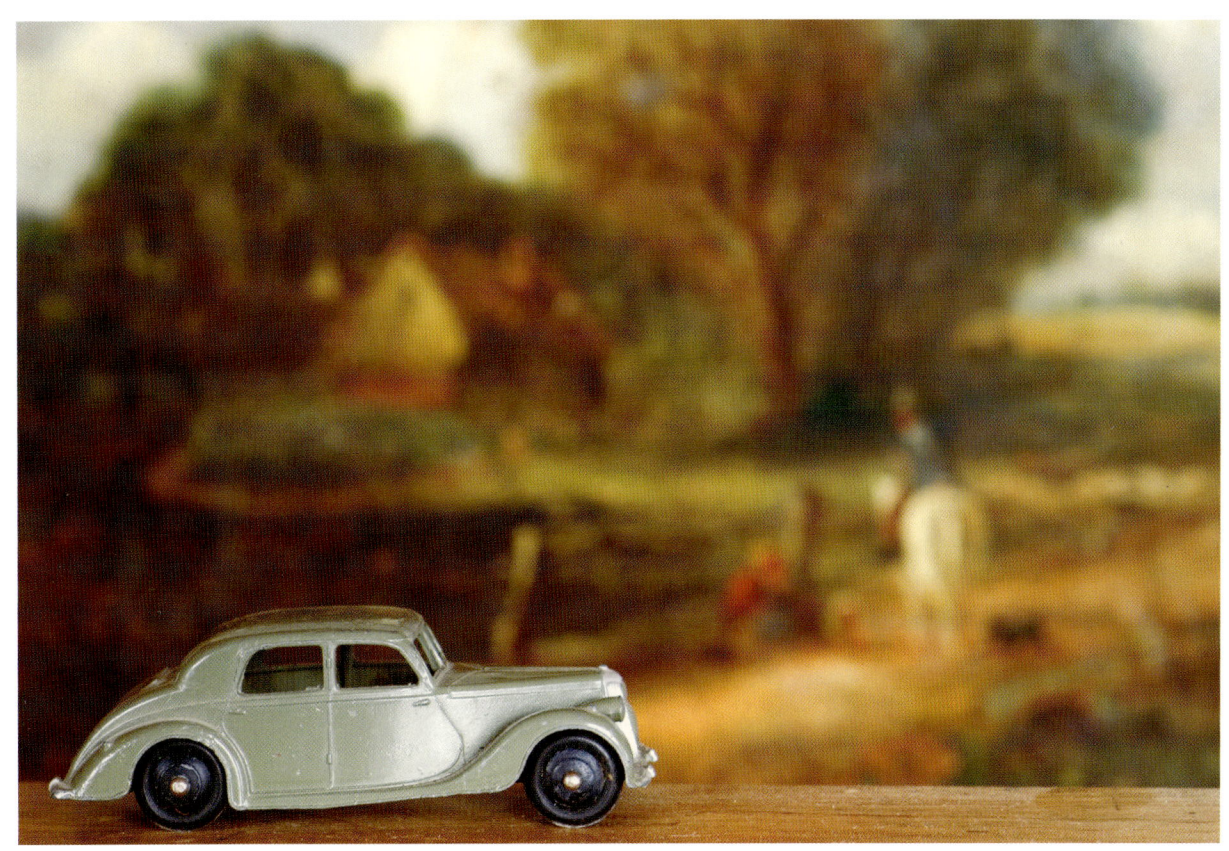

Humber Vogue Saloon, 1937-50.
Re-issue of pre-war 36 series.

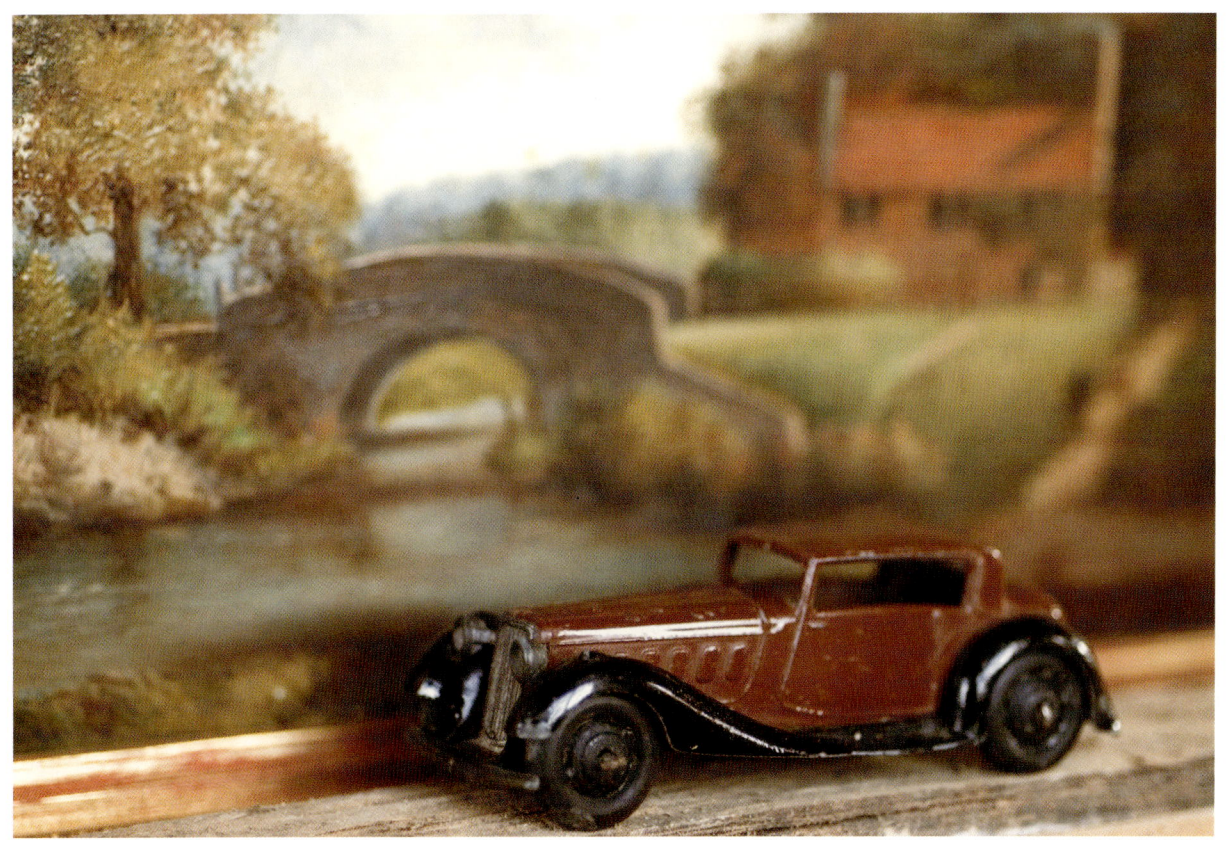

Austin A90 Atlantic, 1951-58.

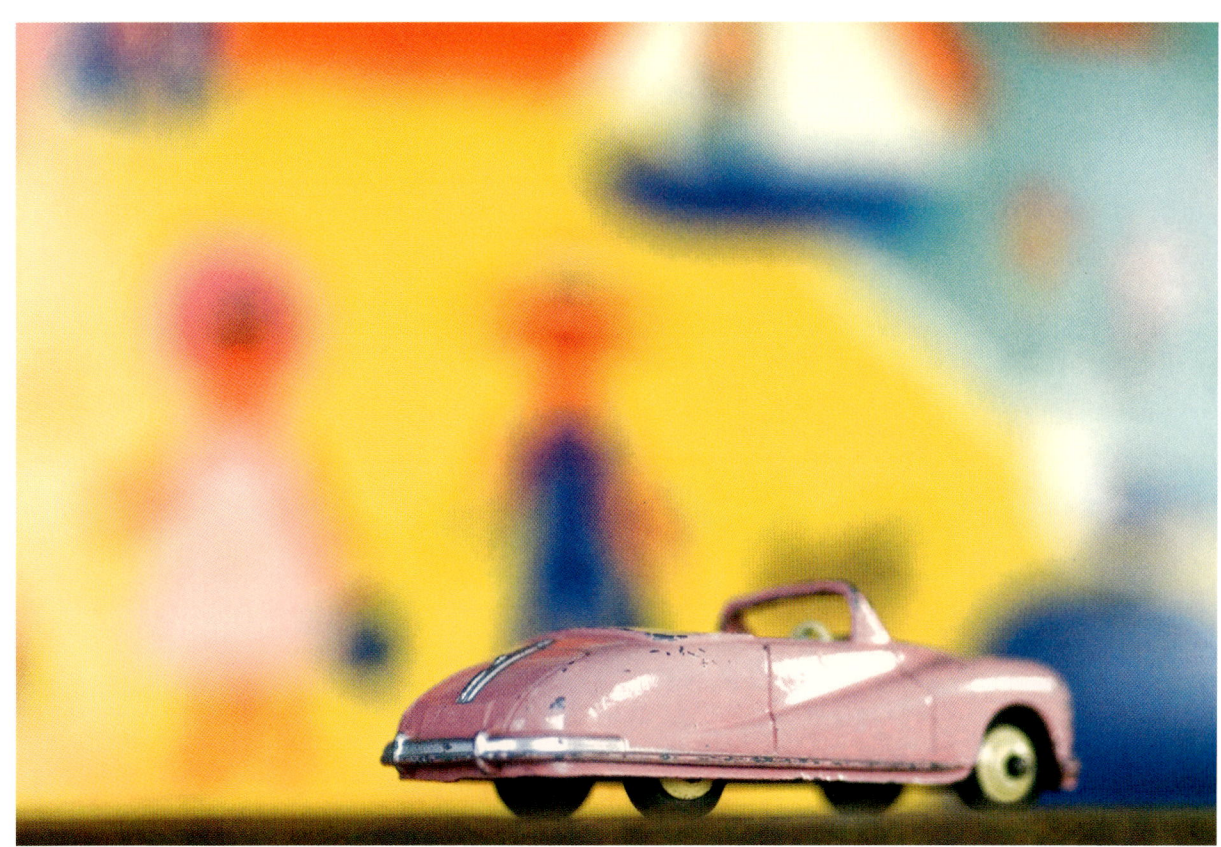

A splendid reproduction of a popular car with a striking horizontal grille. Now available in gay two-colour schemes.

Morris Oxfords, 1950-60.

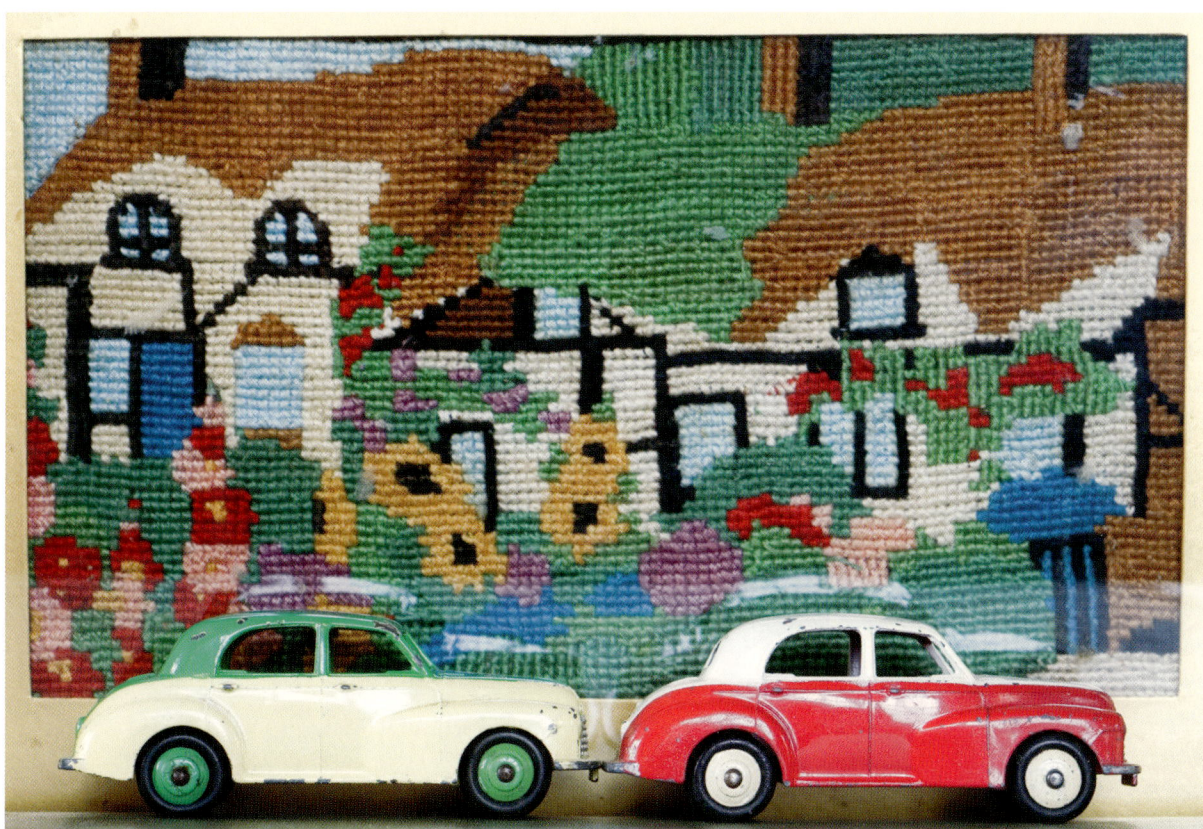

This model is well suited to the up to date two colour finishes.

Austin A40 Somerset, 1954-60.

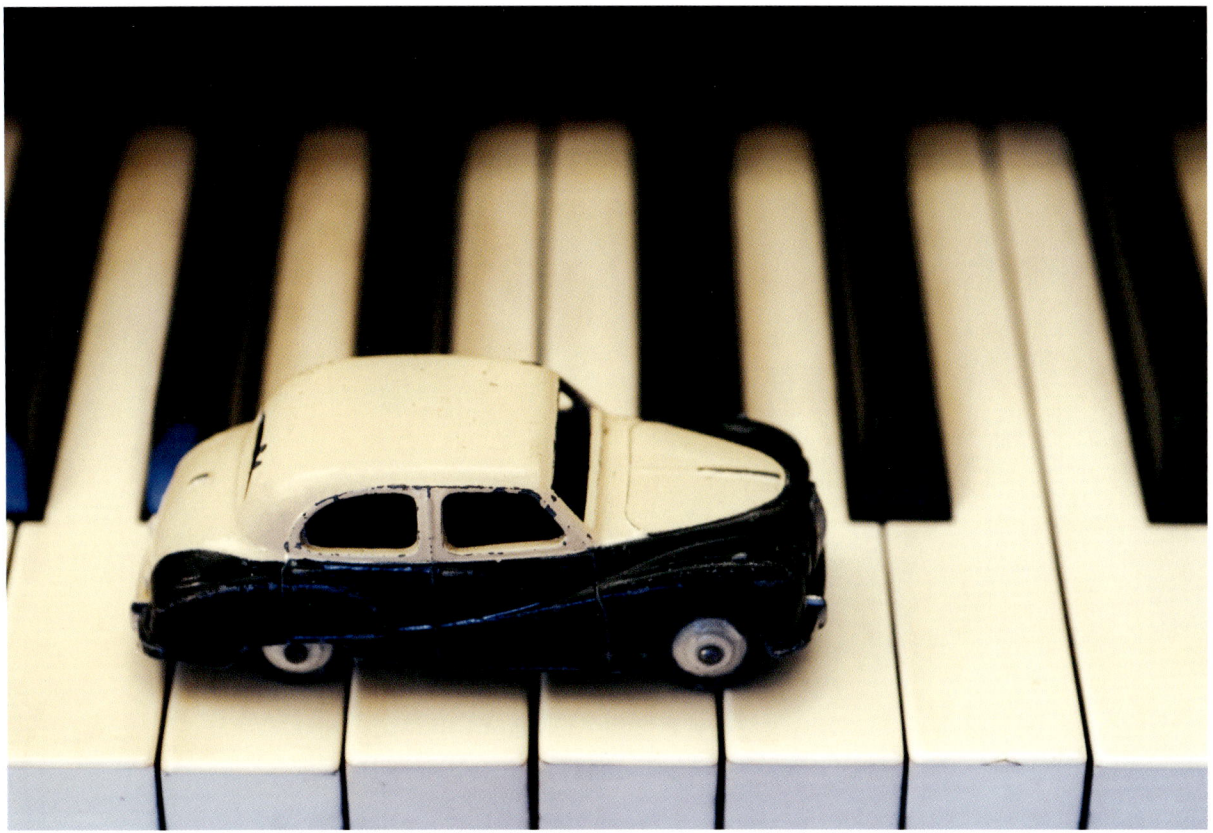

A fine reproduction of a successful modern motor car.

Standard Vanguards, 1948-60.

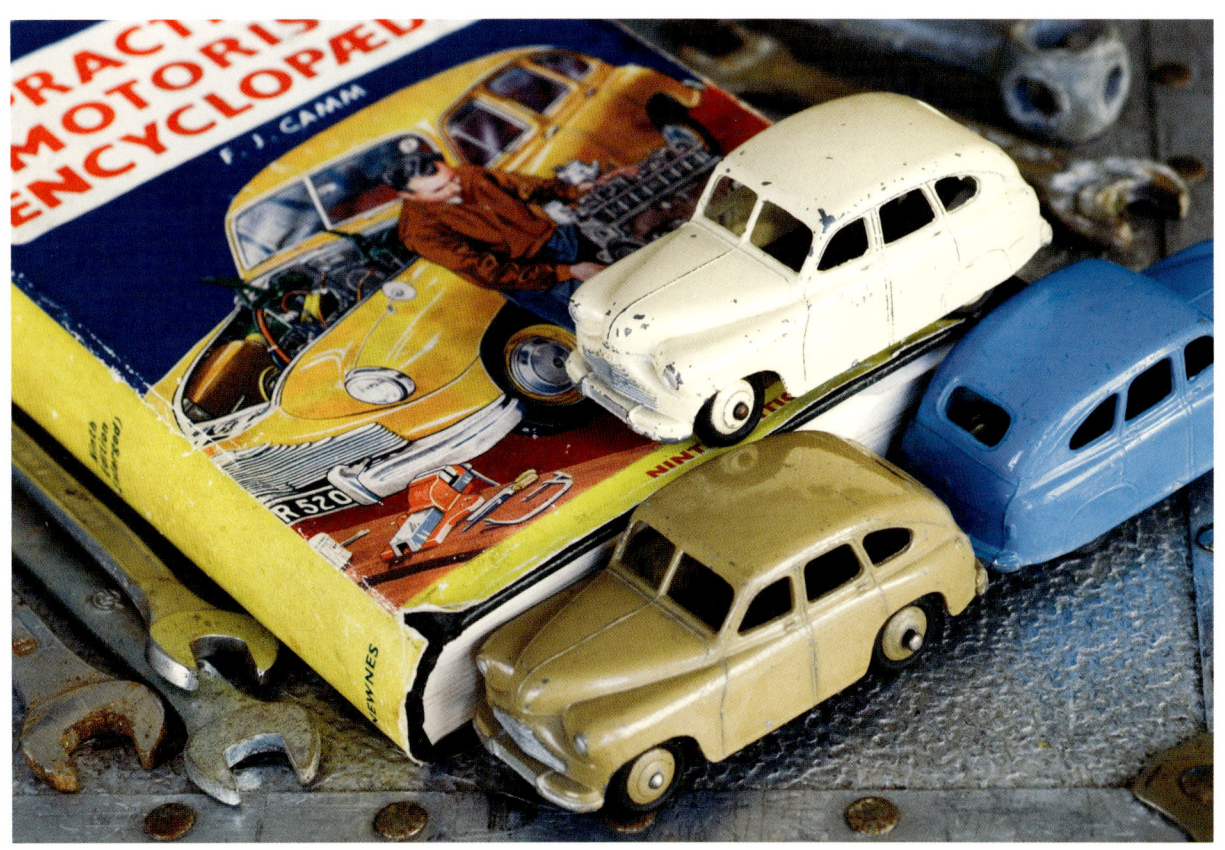

Here is a fine new model, the Humber Police Patrol Car, containing uniformed driver and patrolman.

Humber Hawk Police Car, 1960-64.

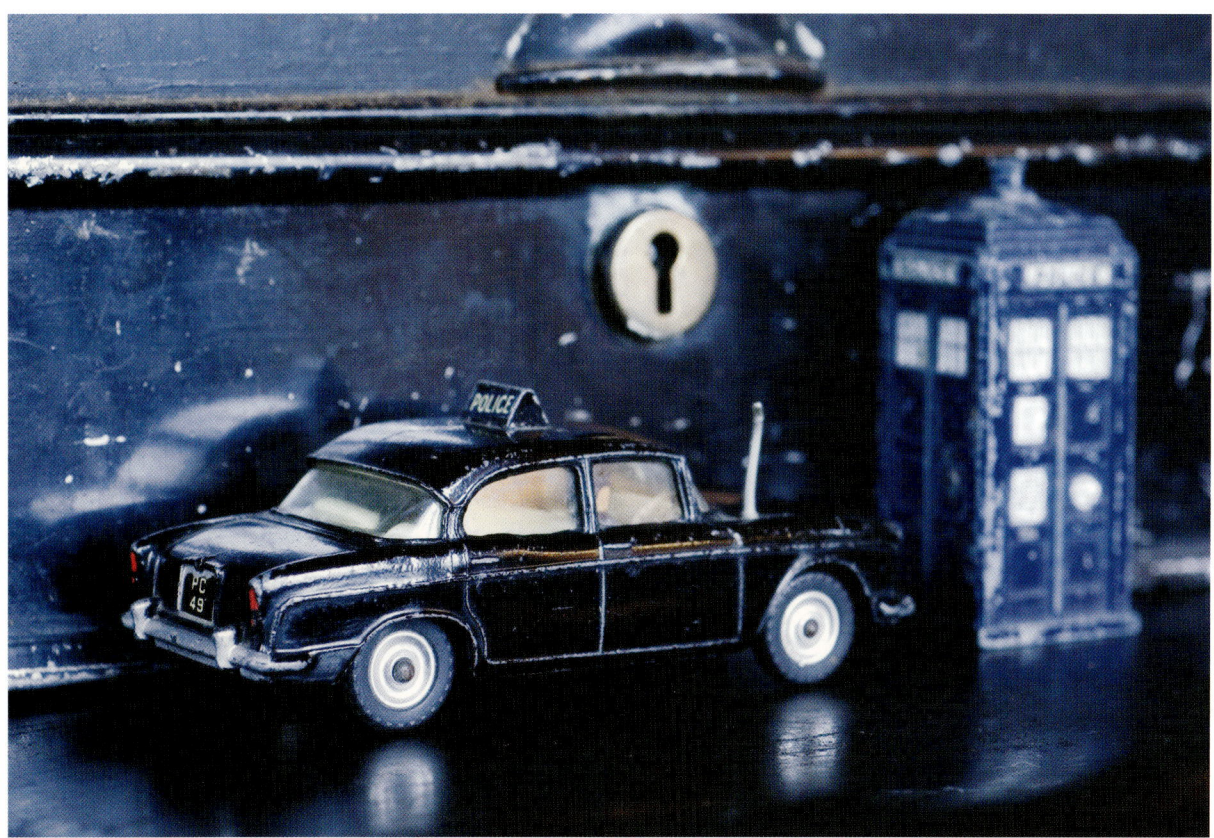

An elegant model of the best car in the world.

Rolls Royce Silver Wraith, 1959-62.

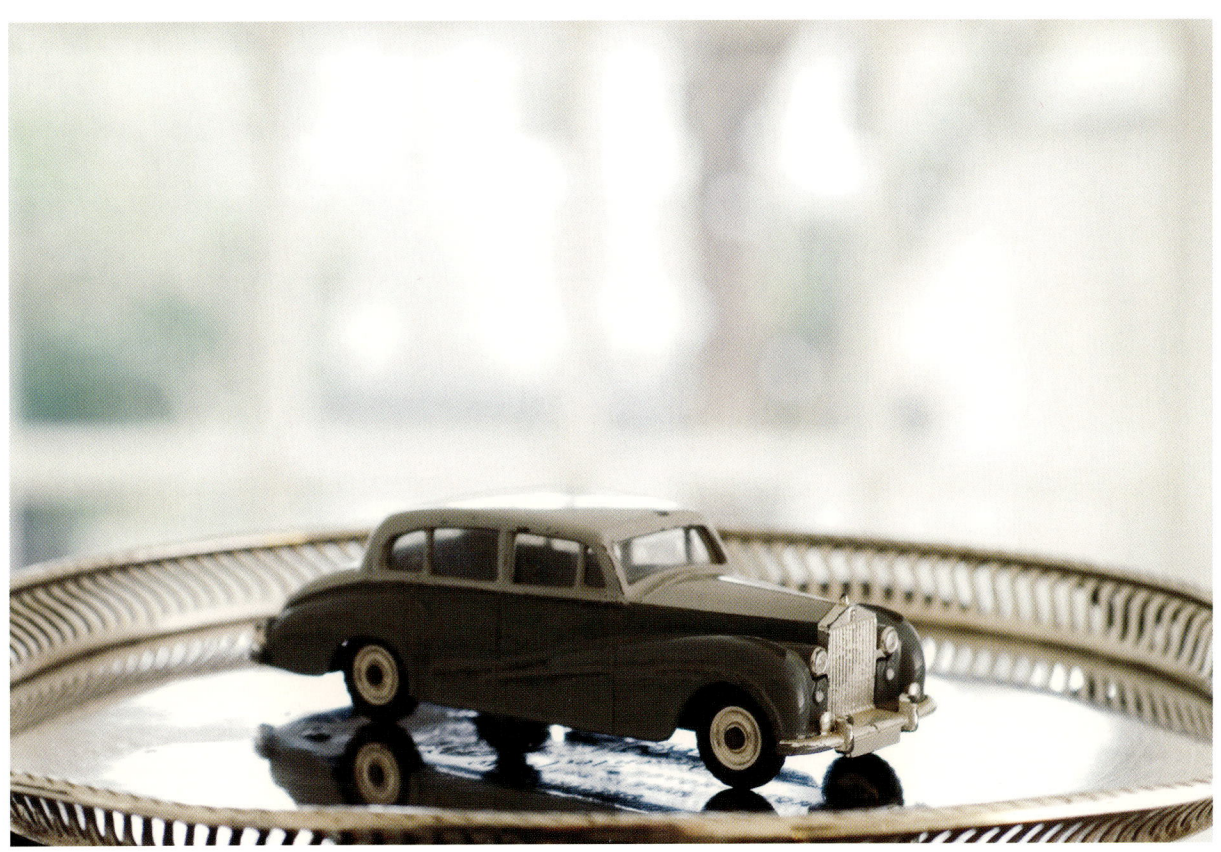

Citroen Traction Avant, 1949-57.
A family saloon car much favoured by
the French Police. Made in France.

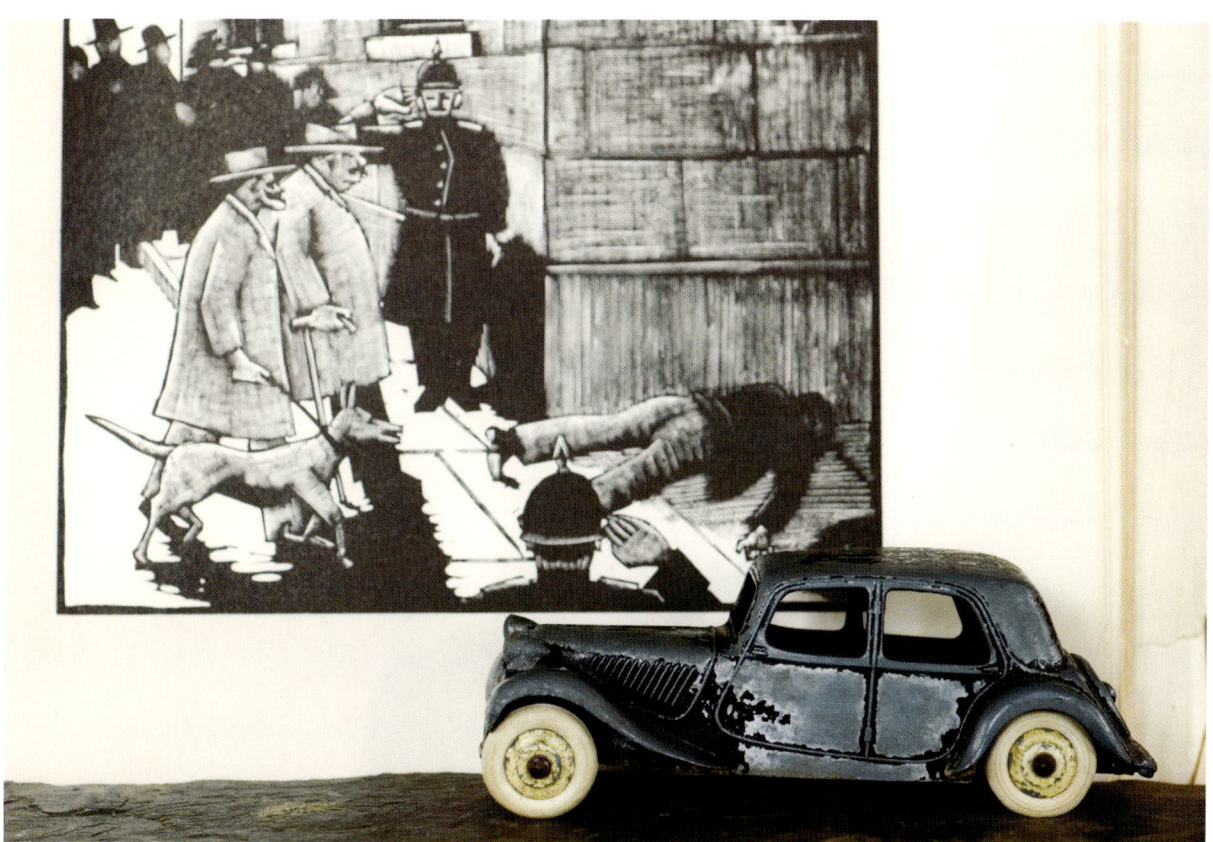

Citroen 2 CV, 1952-59.
Made in France.

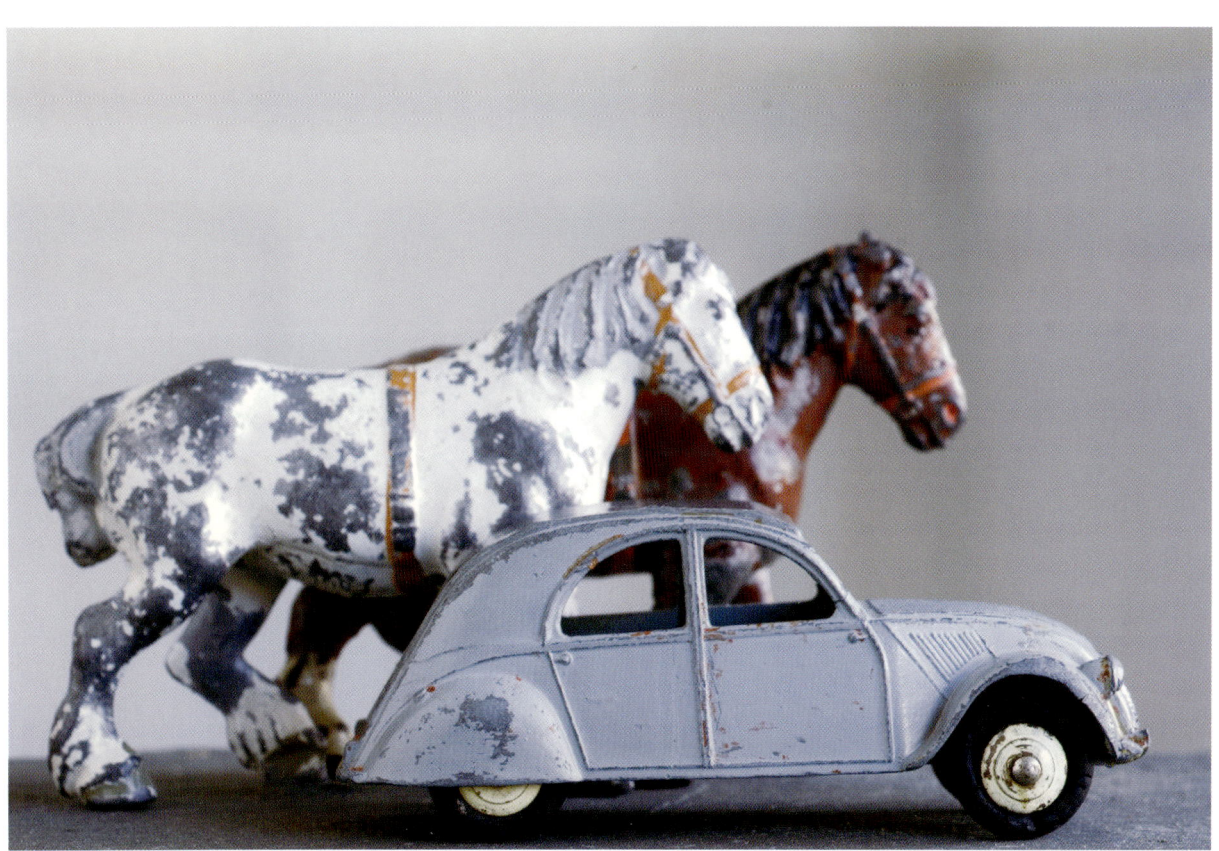

All the character of this roomy, typically-American automobile is captured in the finely detailed Dinky Toys model.

Packard Convertible, 1955-61 (right).

A fascinating and detailed model of the most luxurious cars in the DeSoto range. The clean lines of this powerful car with high-swept tail fins, the bright duo-tone finish, the white tyres and the wrap-around windows are all accurately reproduced in this splendid model.

DeSoto Fireflite, 1958-64 (left).

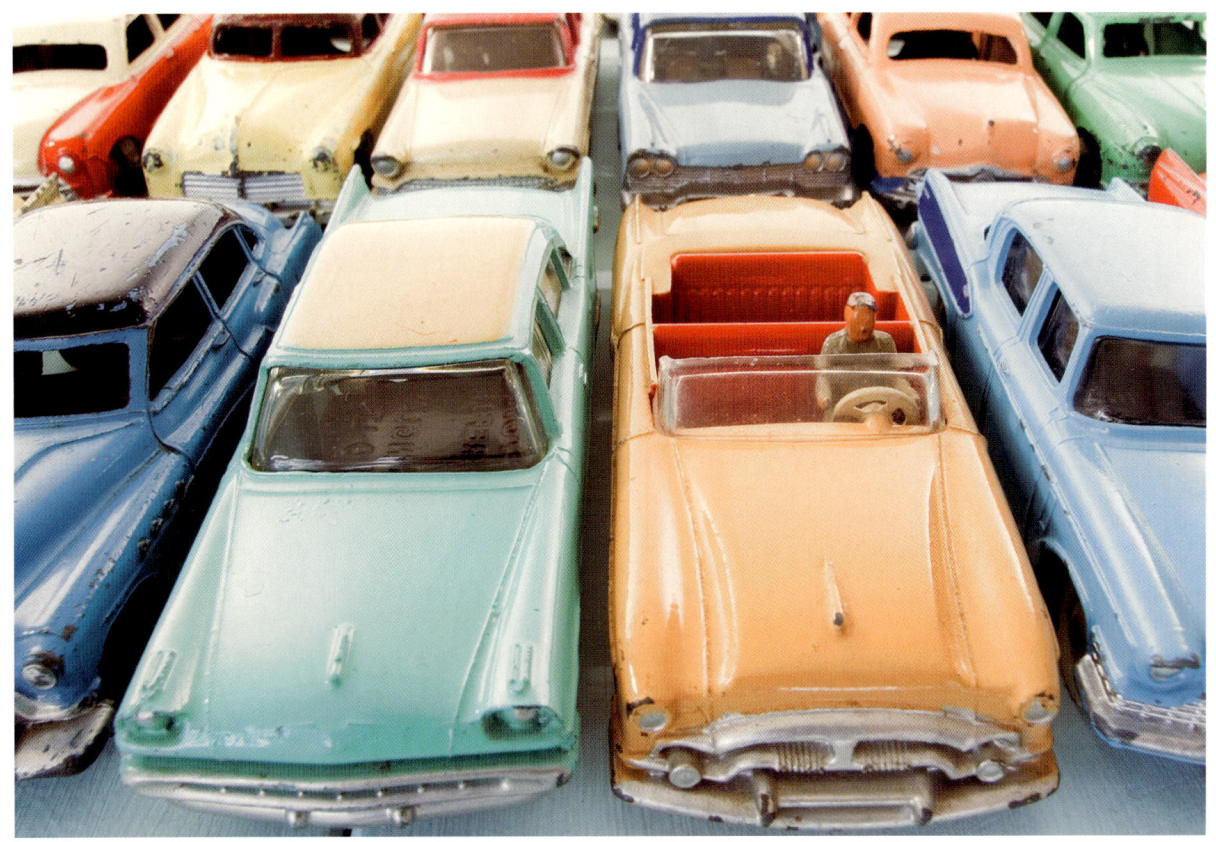

Packard Super 8 Tourer, 1939-50.
Re-issue of pre-war 39 series.

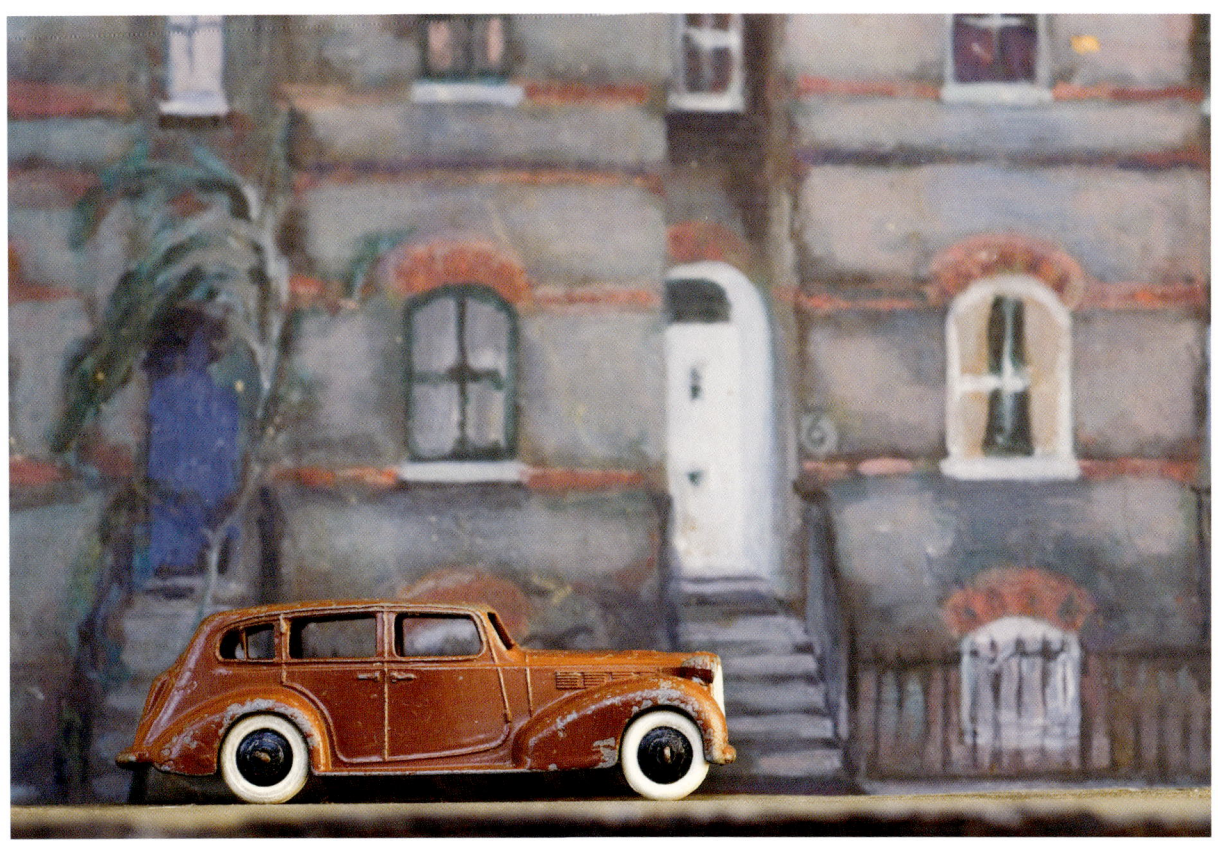

Lincoln Zephyr Coupe, 1939-52.
Re-issue of pre-war 39 series.

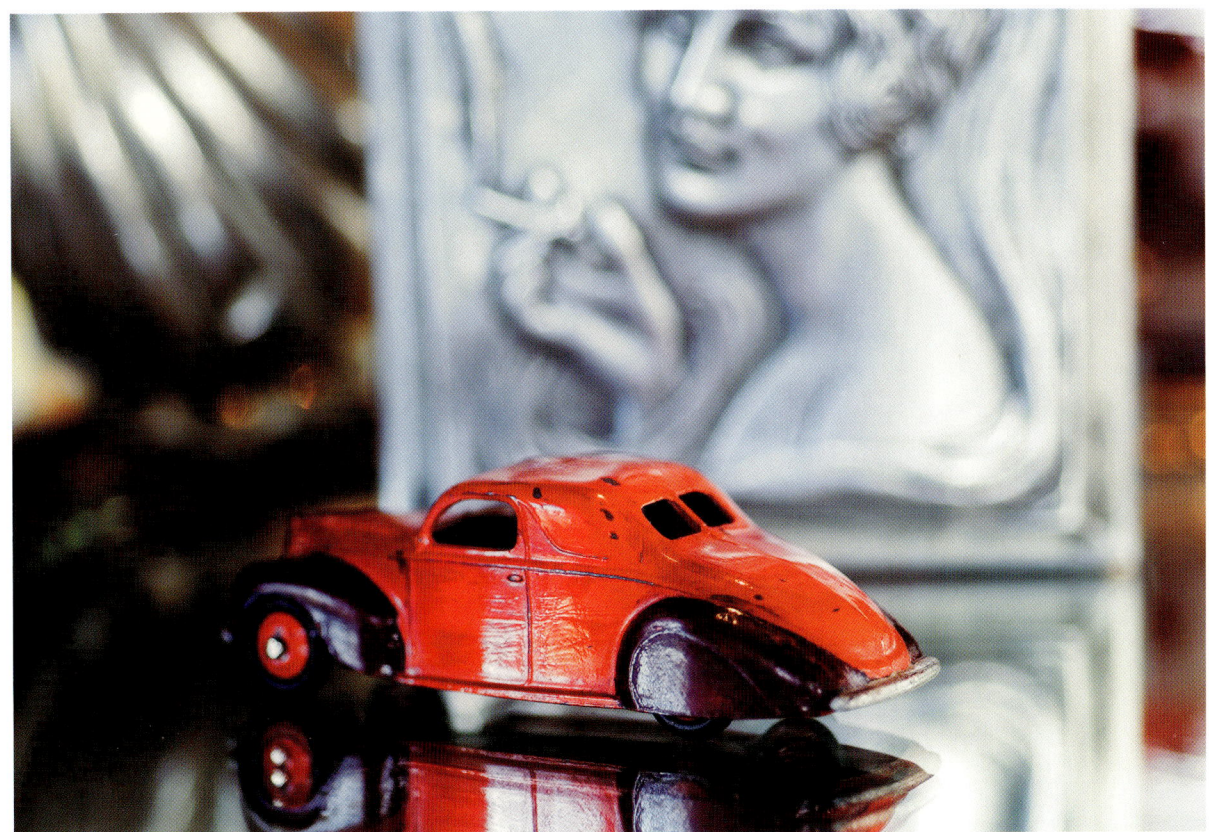

Buick Viceroy Saloon, 1939-50.
Re-issue of pre-war 39 series.

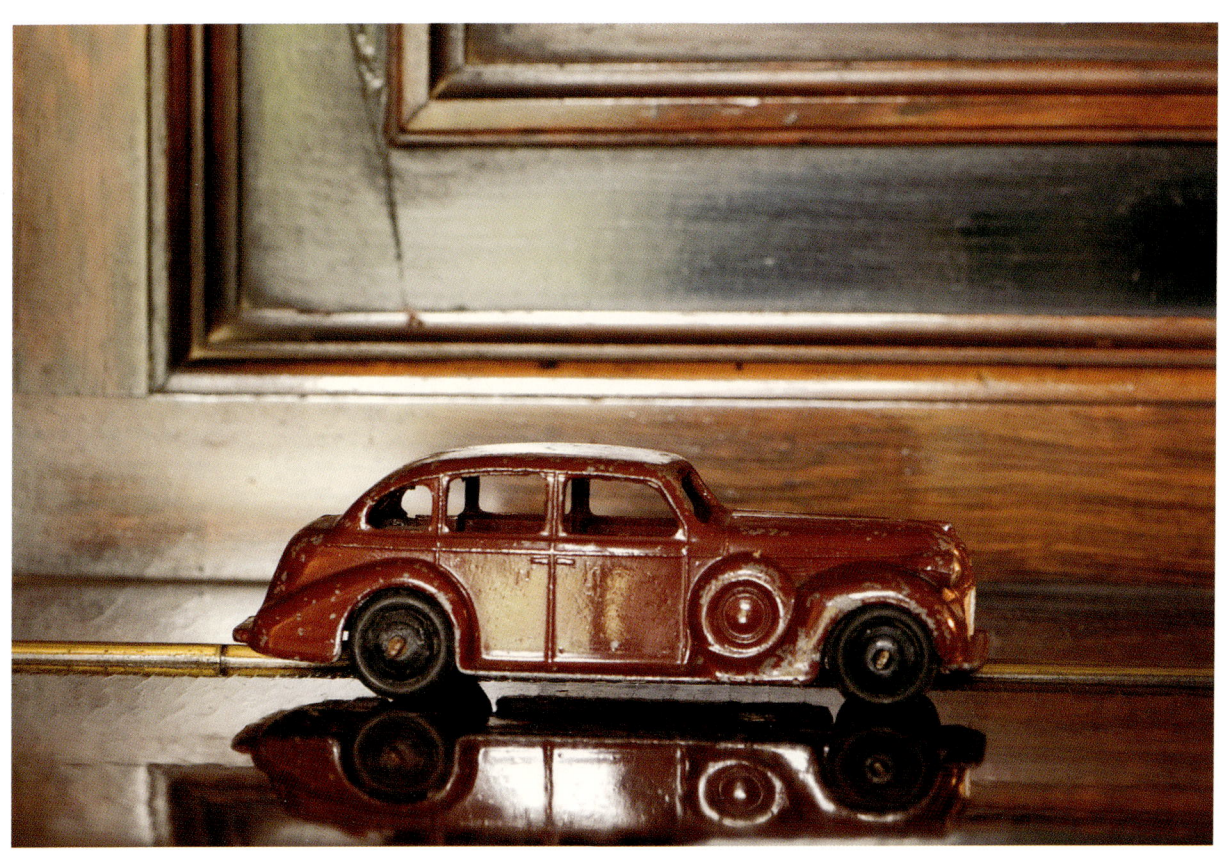

A splendid model of one of America's fastest and most famous roadsters.

Cadillac Eldorado, 1956-63.

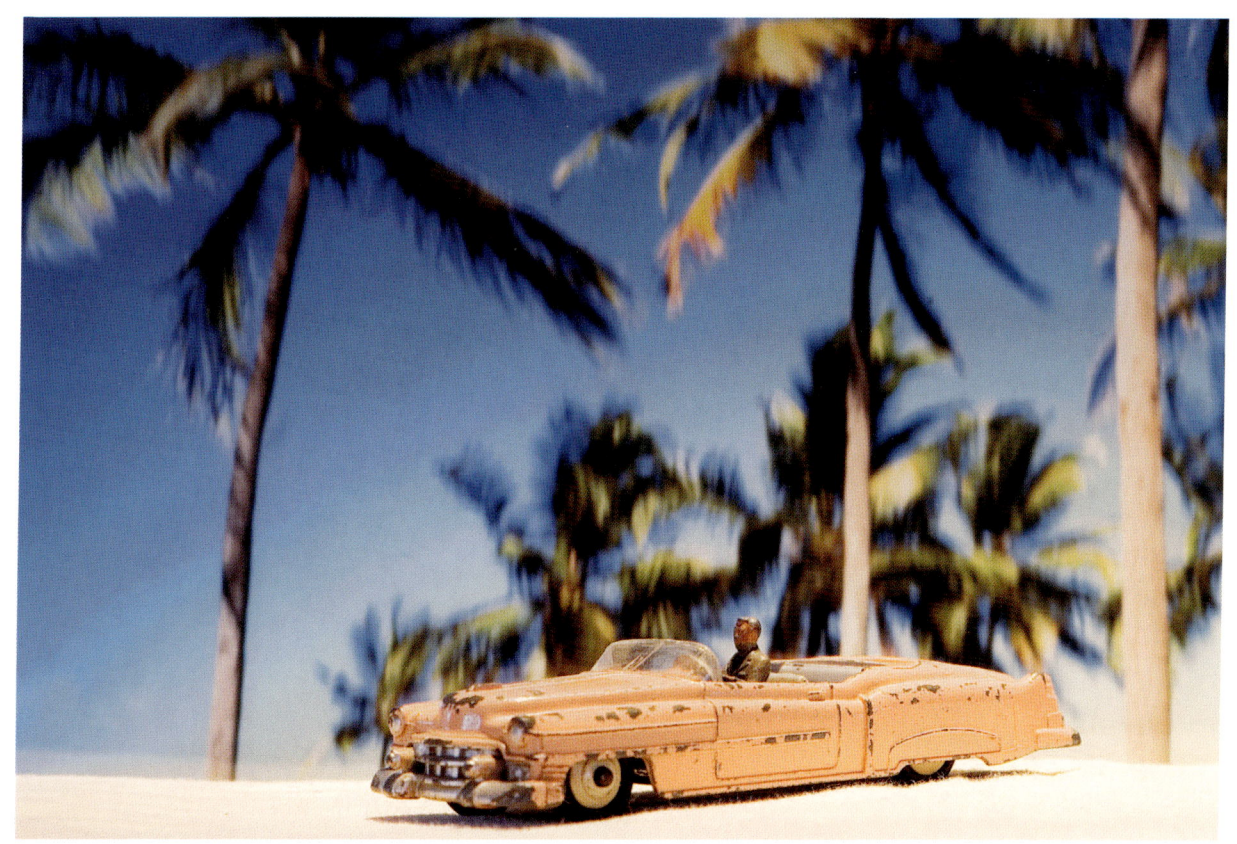

This superbly detailed model reproduces the sleek surging lines with an accuracy that will delight the enthusiast.

Studebaker Golden Hawk, 1958-63.

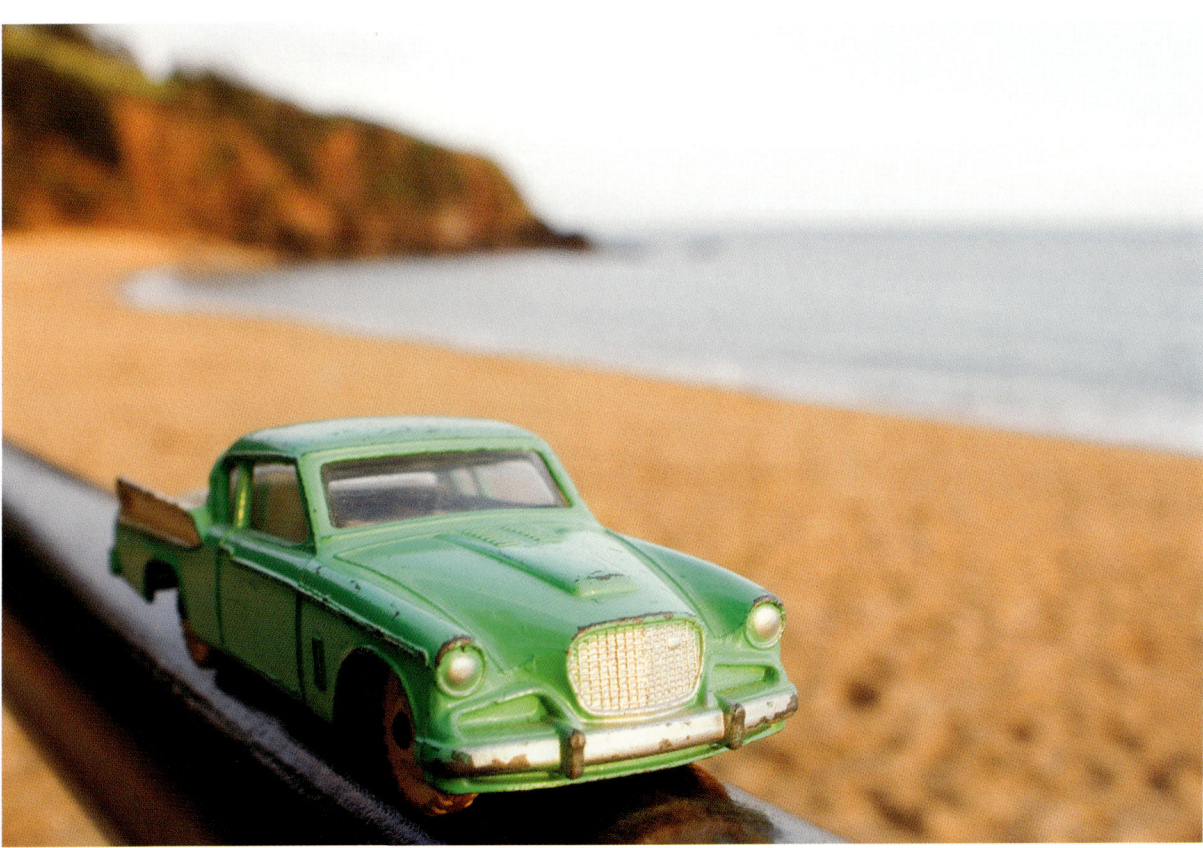

These American cars are large handsome vehicles now available in a choice of striking two-colour schemes.

Ford Fordors, 1949-59.

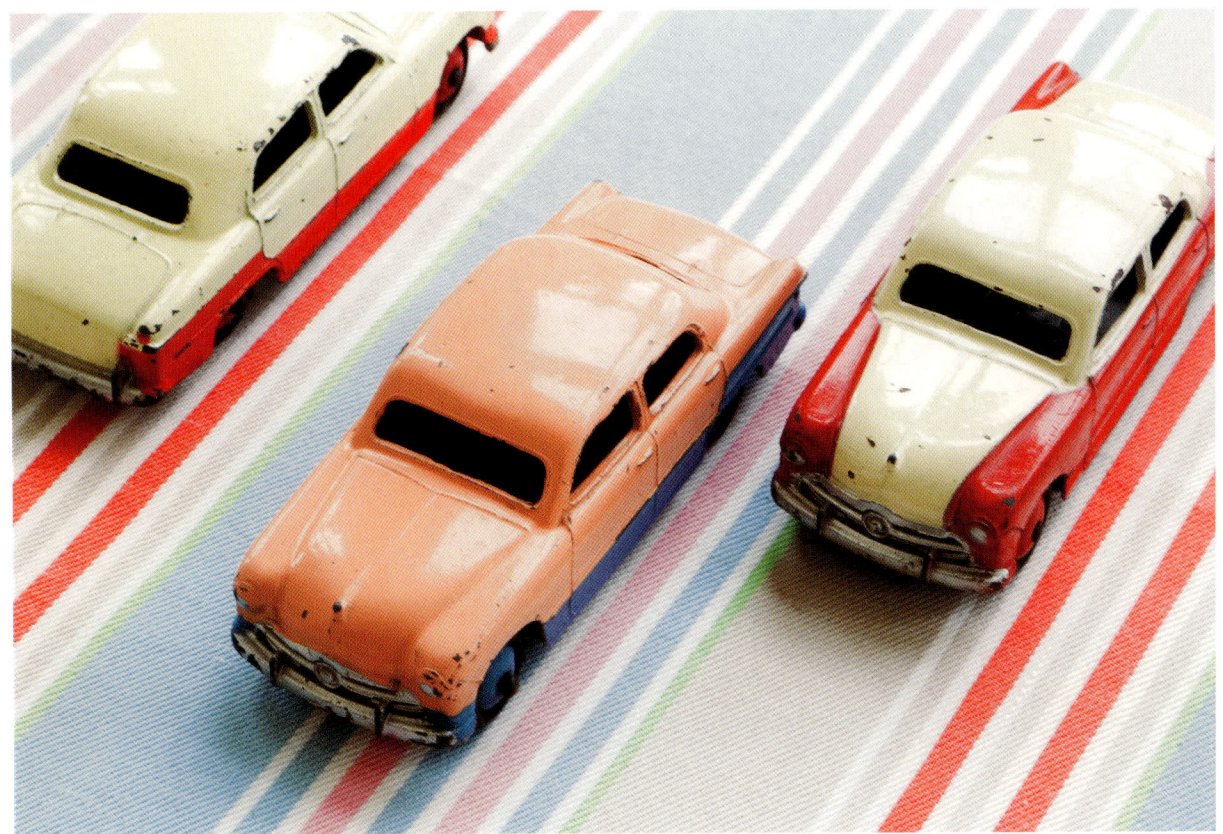

This typically American automobile is fitted with driver and moulded plastic windscreen.

Packard Convertible, 1955-61.

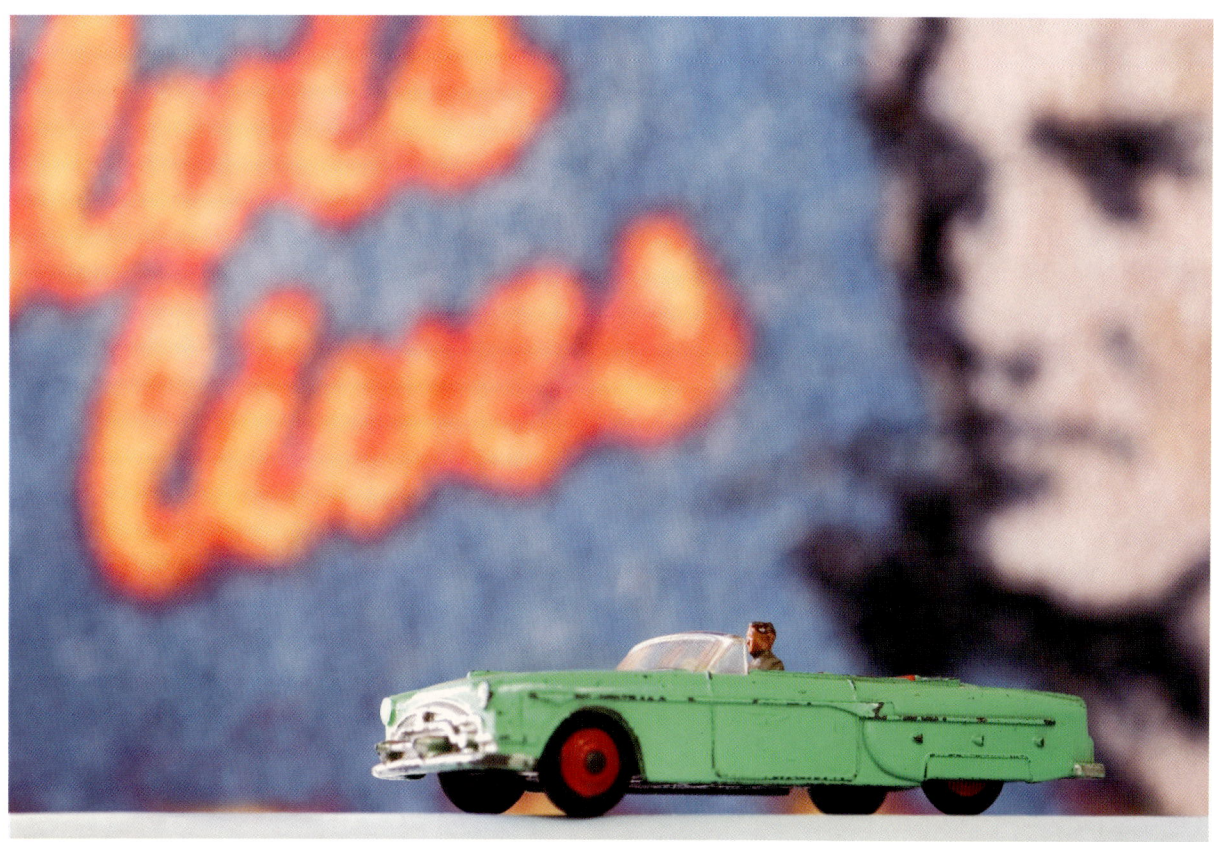

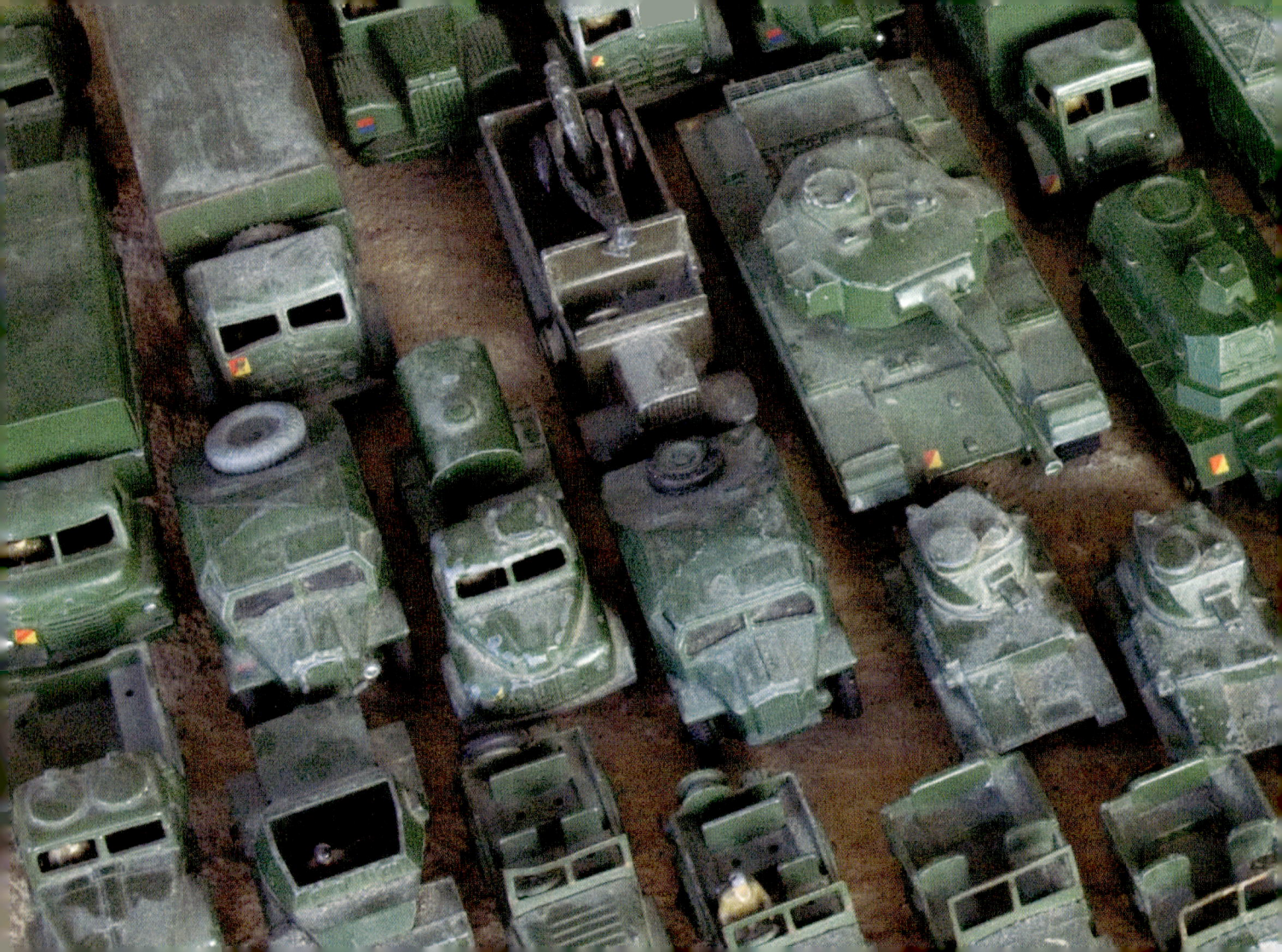

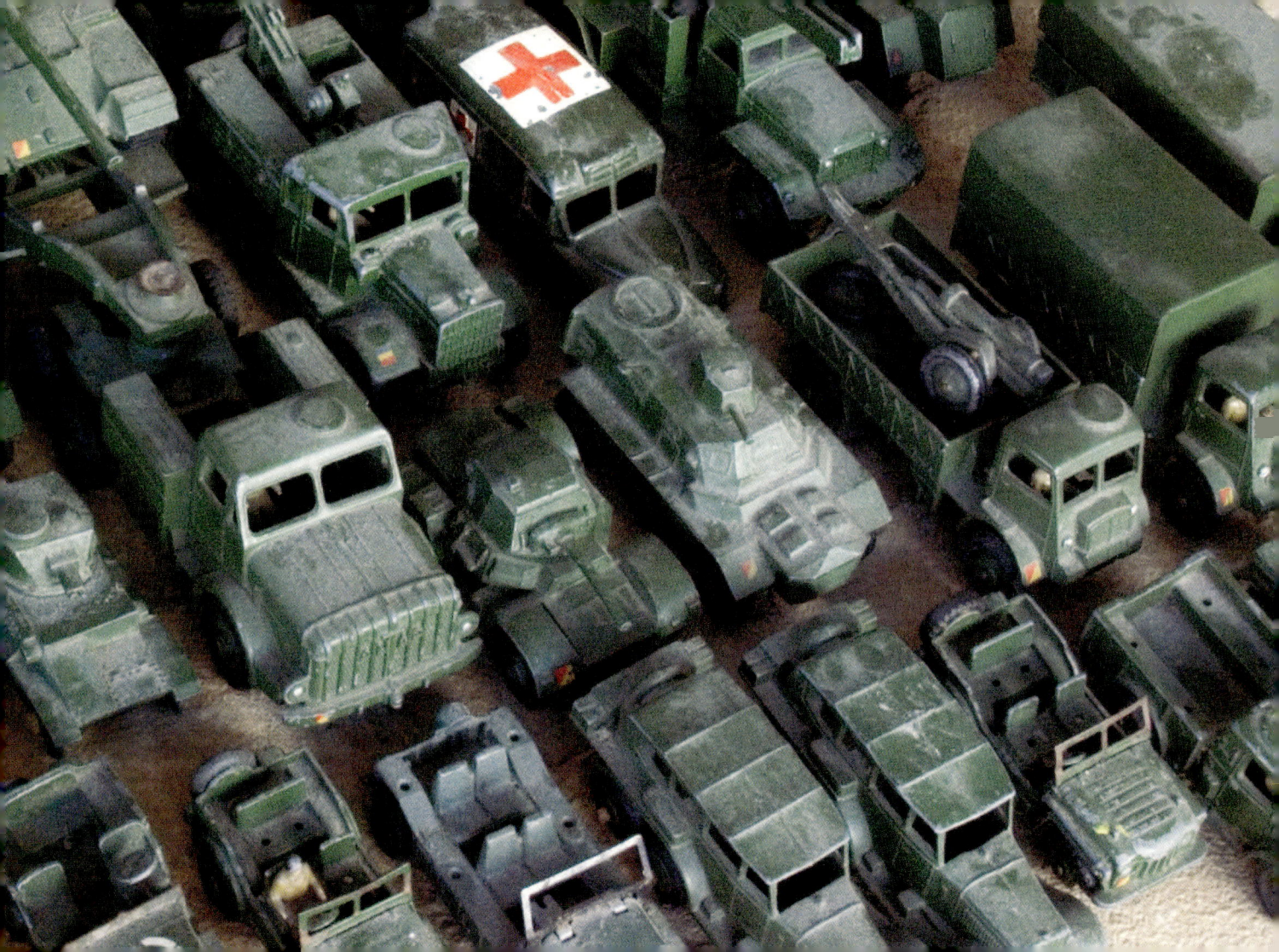

A wonderfully realistic miniature of the most famous car in the war.

US Jeep, 1946-54.
First new Dinky casting after the Second World War.

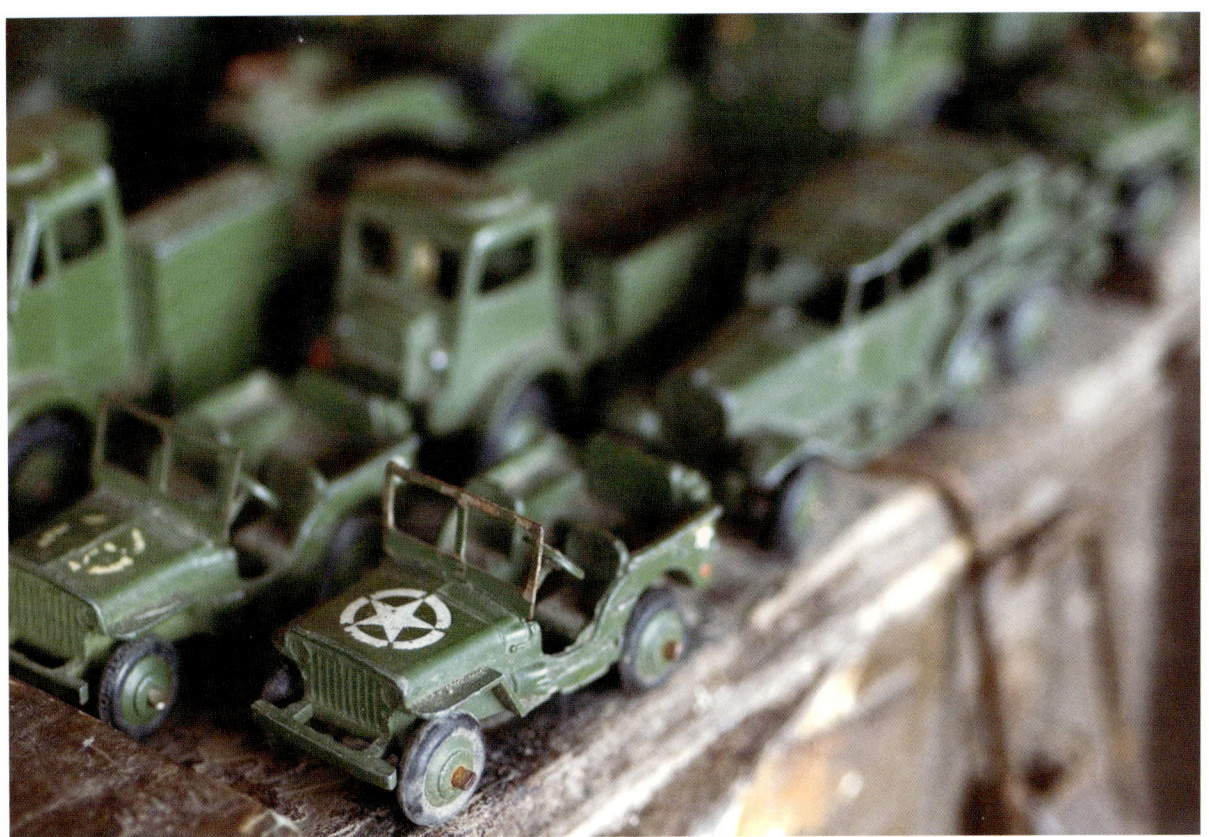

This exciting model of Britain's famous Centurion Tank is a welcome reinforcement for the playroom army.

Centurion Tank, 1954-70.

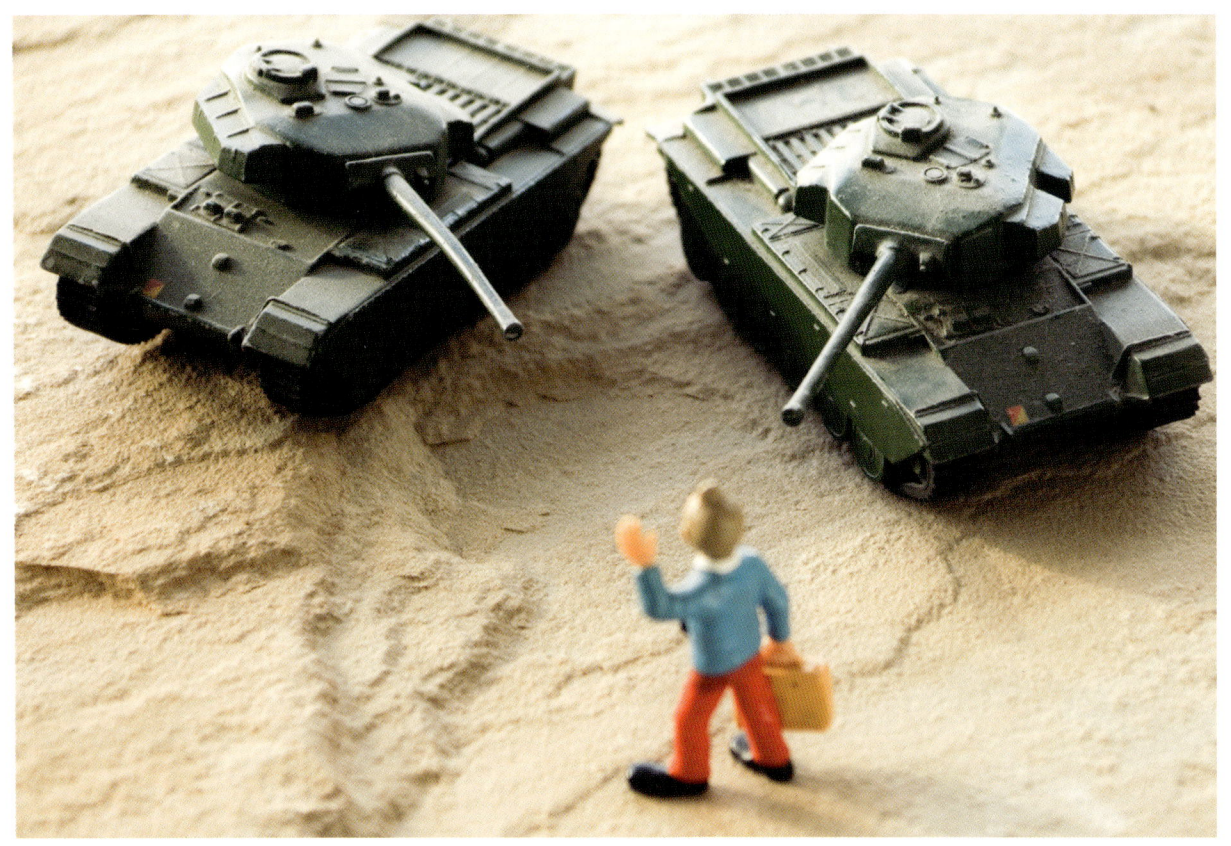

Streamlined Fire Engine, 1936-62. Longest production Dinky.
Re-issue of pre-war 25 series.

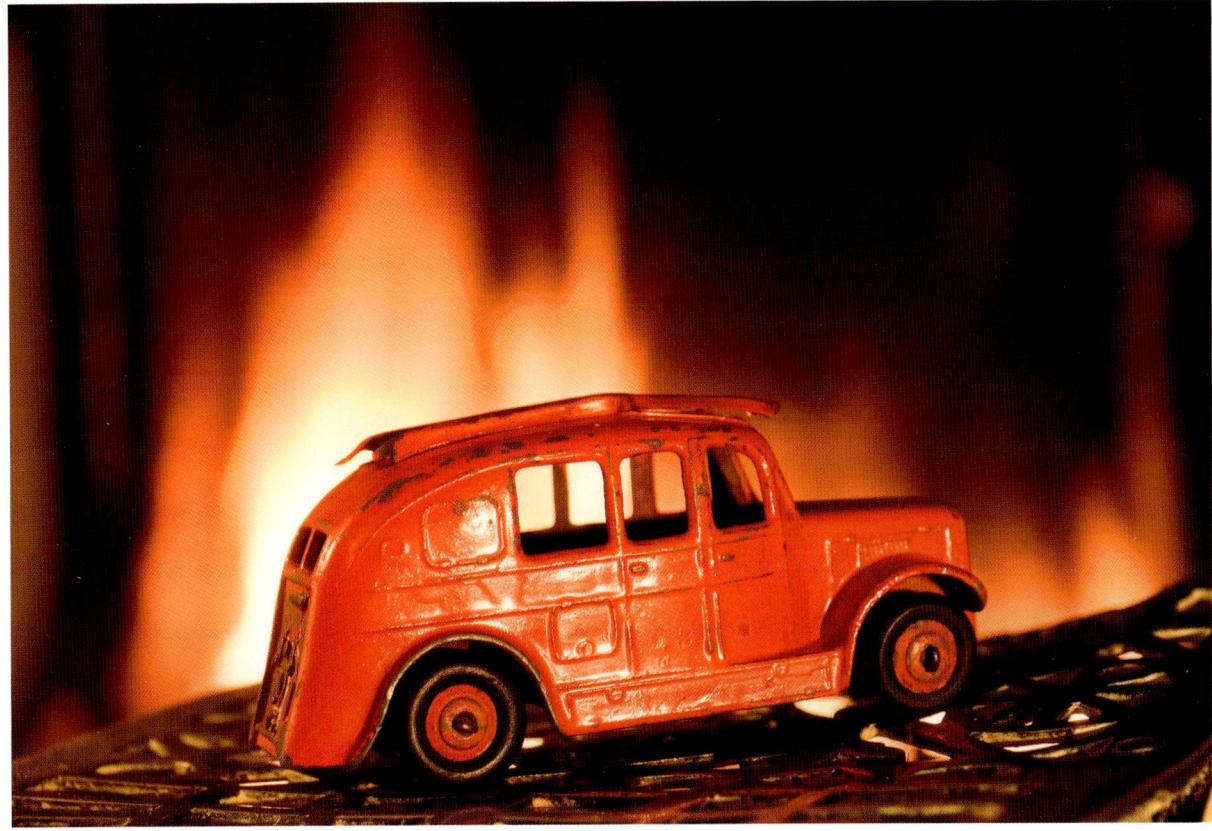

A beautiful model finished in cream with red wheels and The Red Cross on both sides.

Ambulance, 1935-48.
Re-issue of pre-war 30 series.

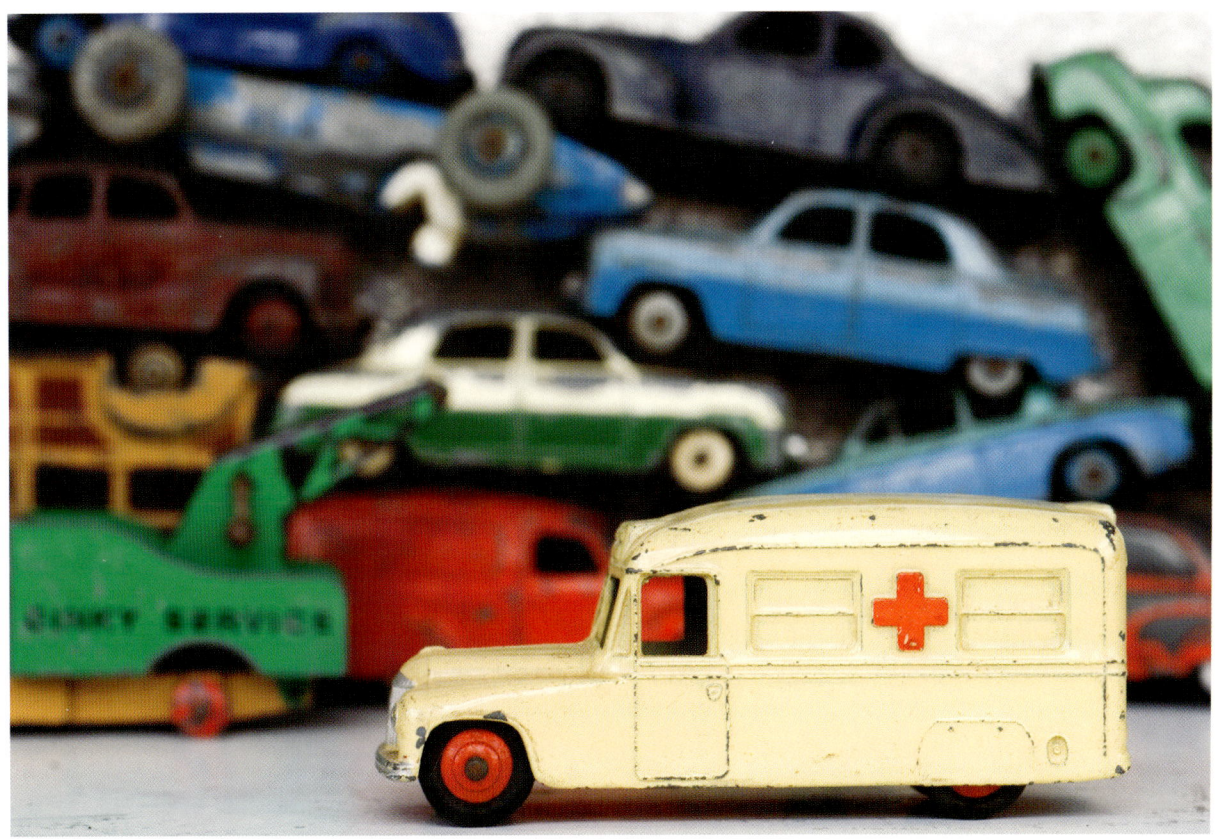

This splendid model is fitted with a robust crane.

Breakdown Lorry, 1935-48.
Re-issue of pre-war 30 series.

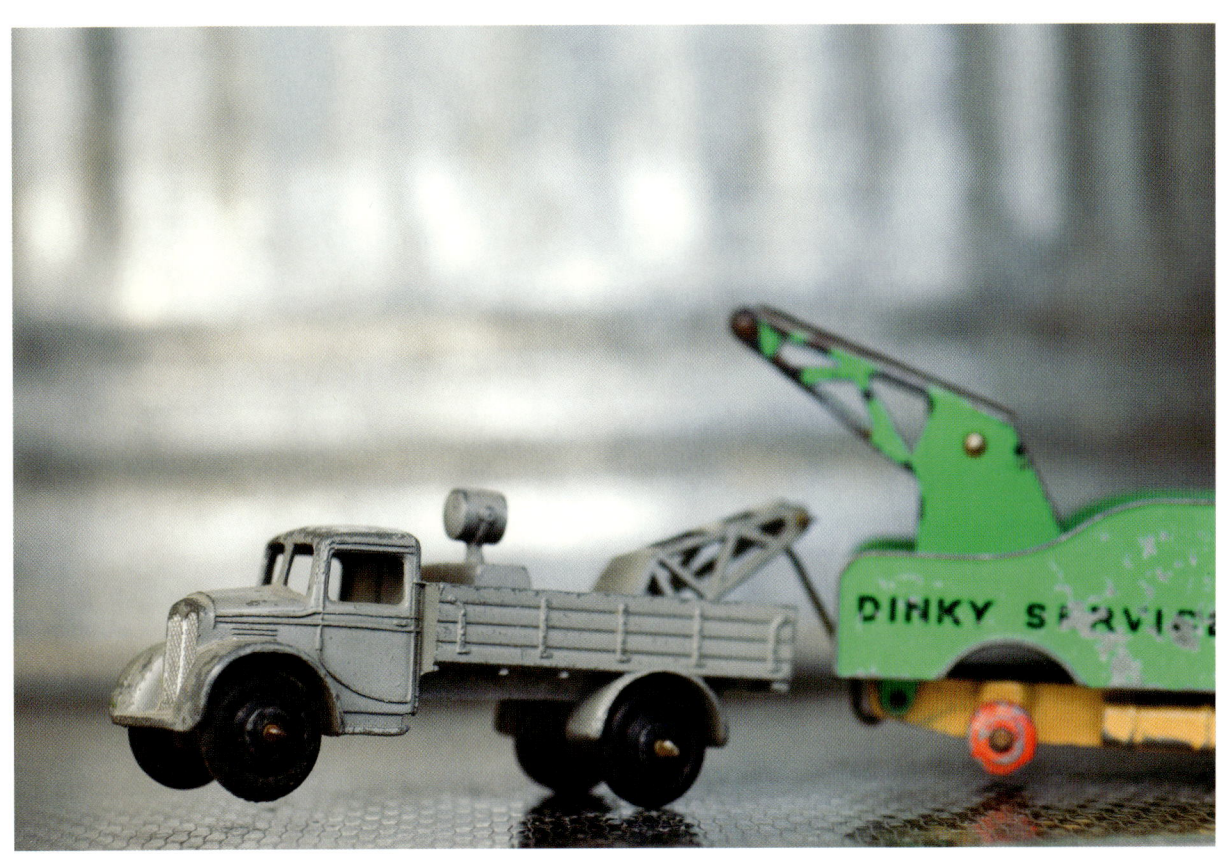

This fine model has hoisting, jib raising and slewing movements.

Coles Mobile Crane, 1949-65.

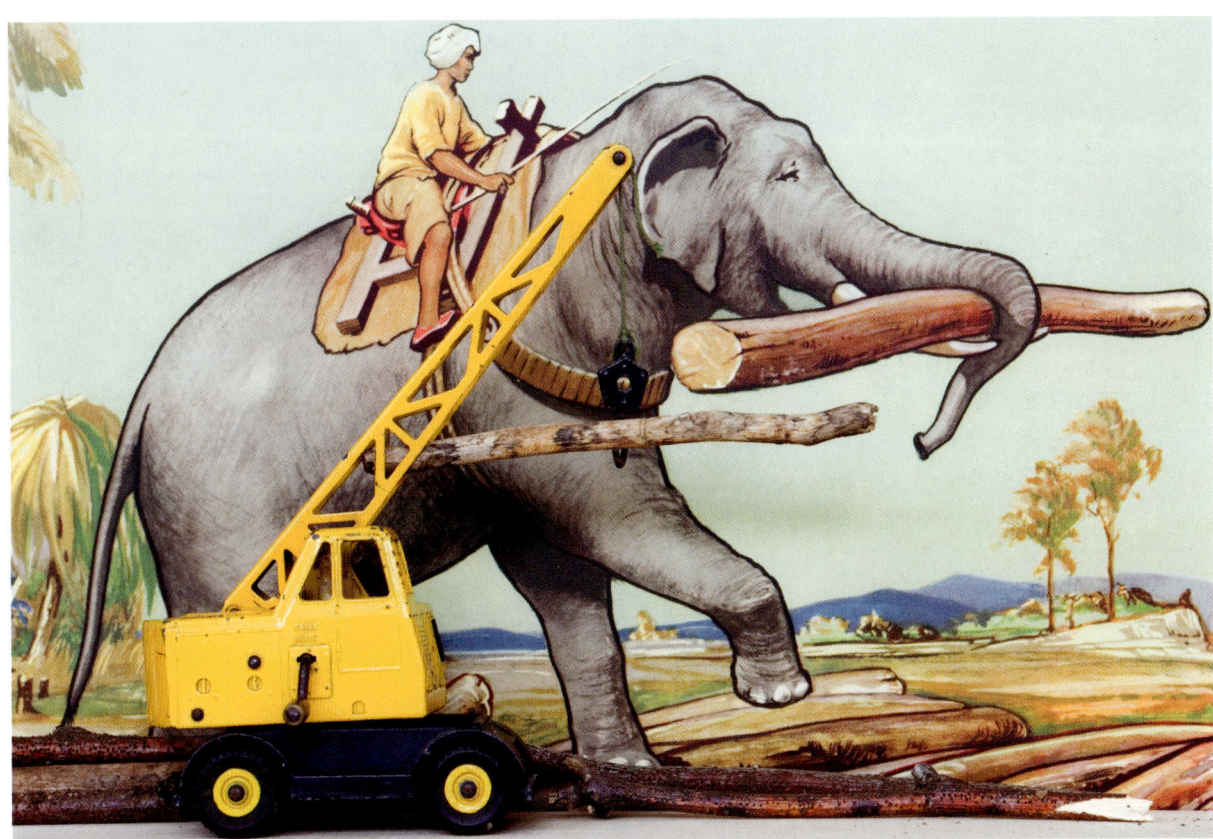

The loading carriage is raised by turning a handle.

Coventry Climax Fork Lift Truck, 1949-64.

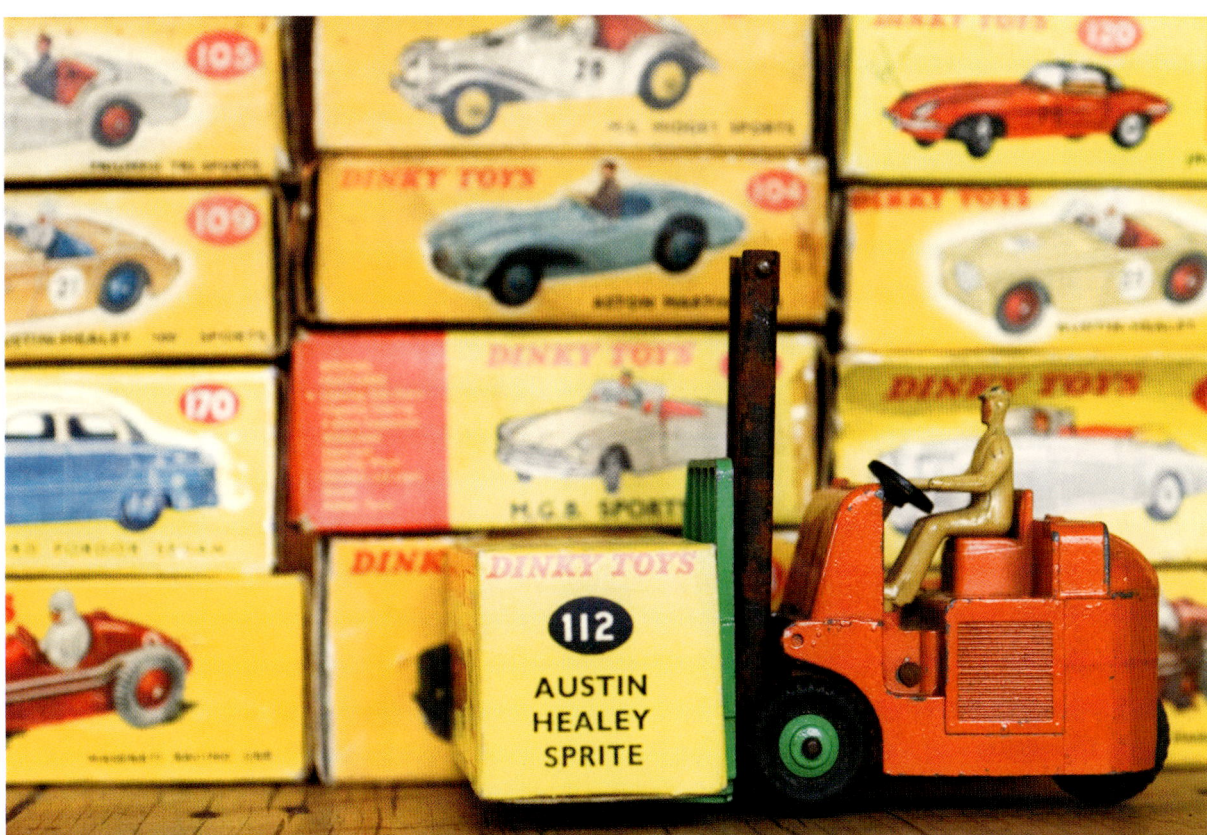

This electric model is a life like reproduction, every important external feature is clearly displayed.

BEV Electric Truck, 1948-60.

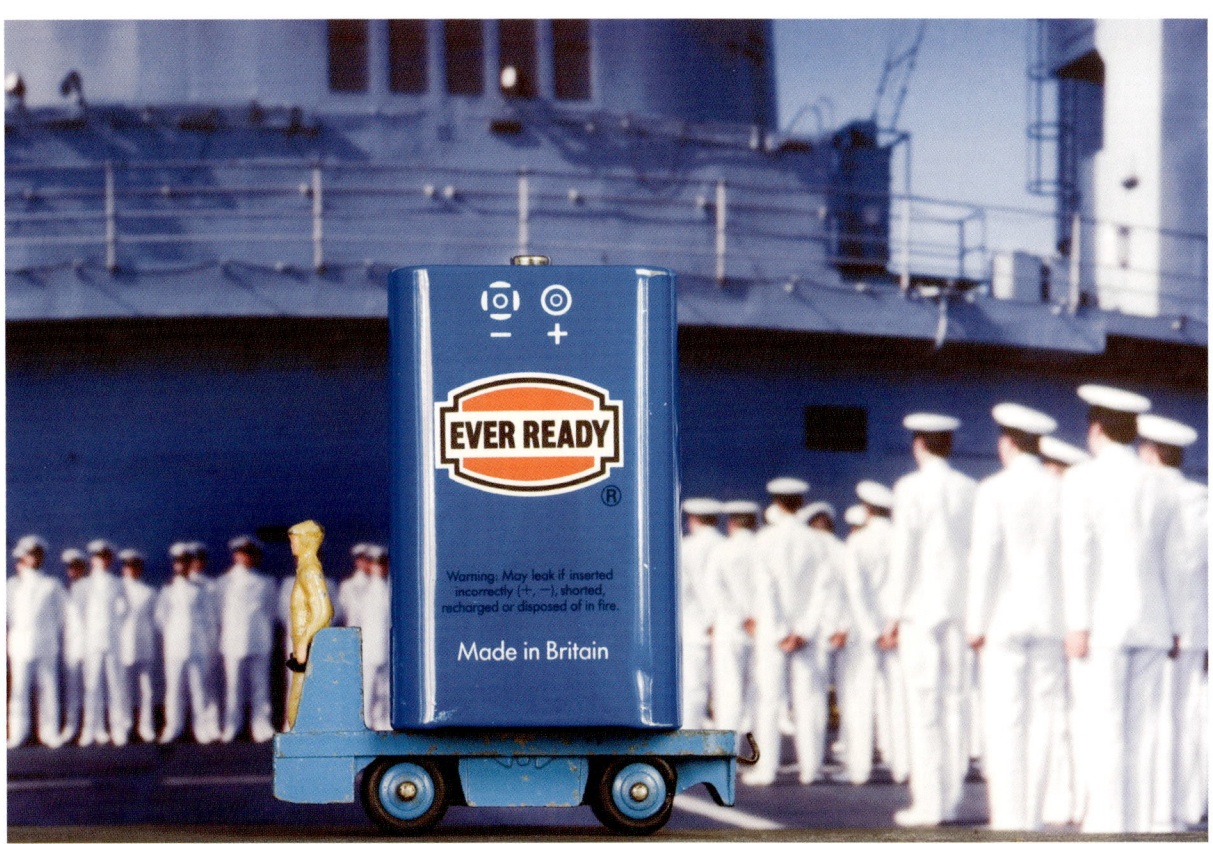

A fine model of a vehicle designed to go anywhere and do anything.

Land Rover, 1950-70.

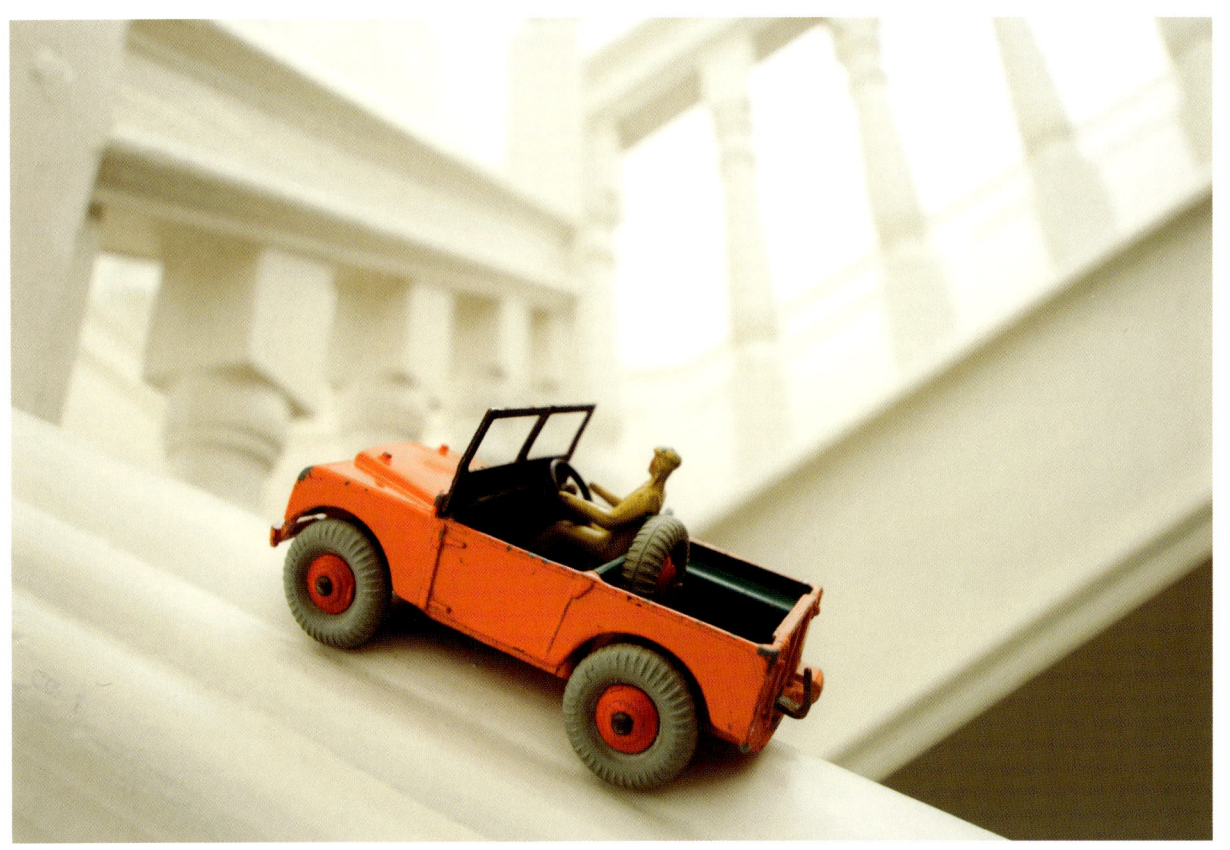

Attractive model of an all purpose farm wagon.

Farm Produce Wagon, 1950-64.

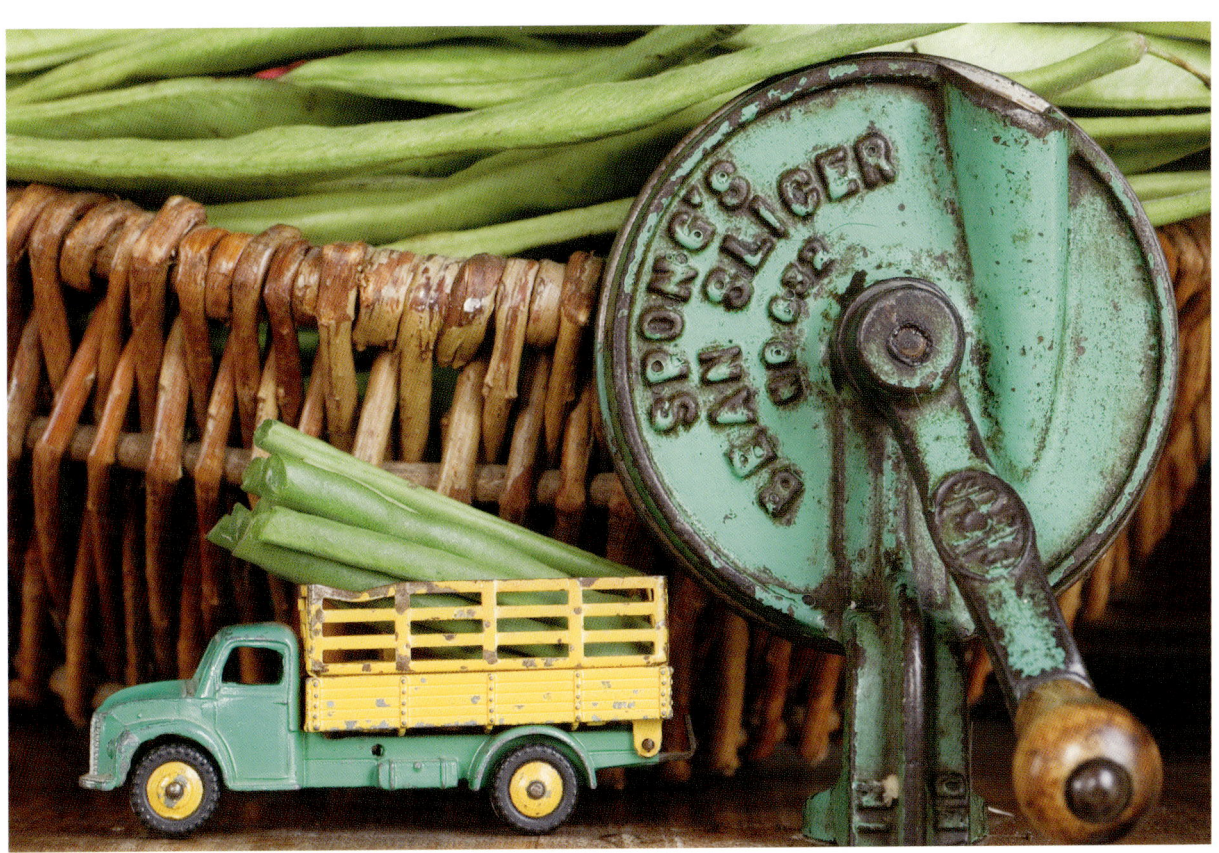

This model is an excellent miniature, perfectly proportioned, accurately detailed and complete with driver.

Field Marshall Tractor, 1953-65.

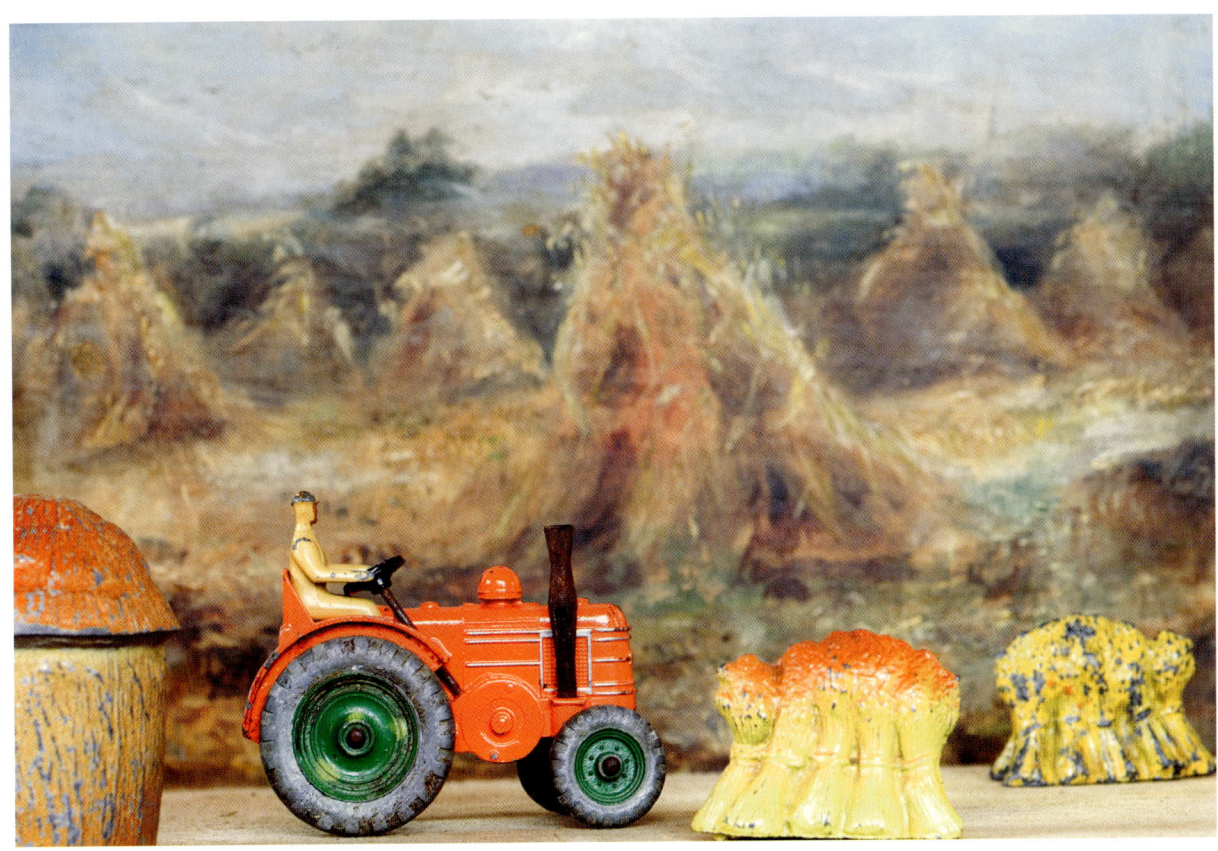

Built for tough work this big, sturdy truck will carry varied loads.

Leyland Comet Lorry, 1949-59.

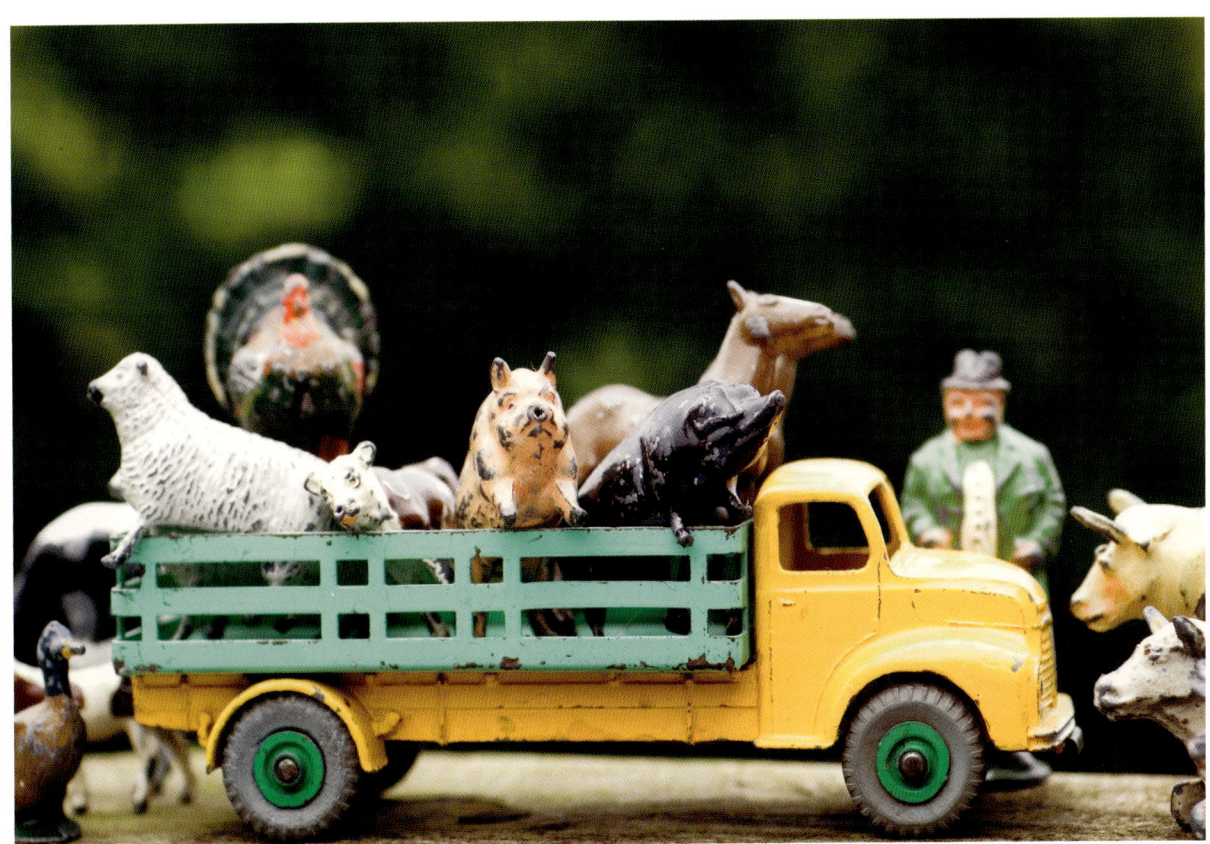

*The finishing touch to this fine model is provided by
the driver, seated correctly at the wheel.*

Massey Harris Tractor, 1948-71.

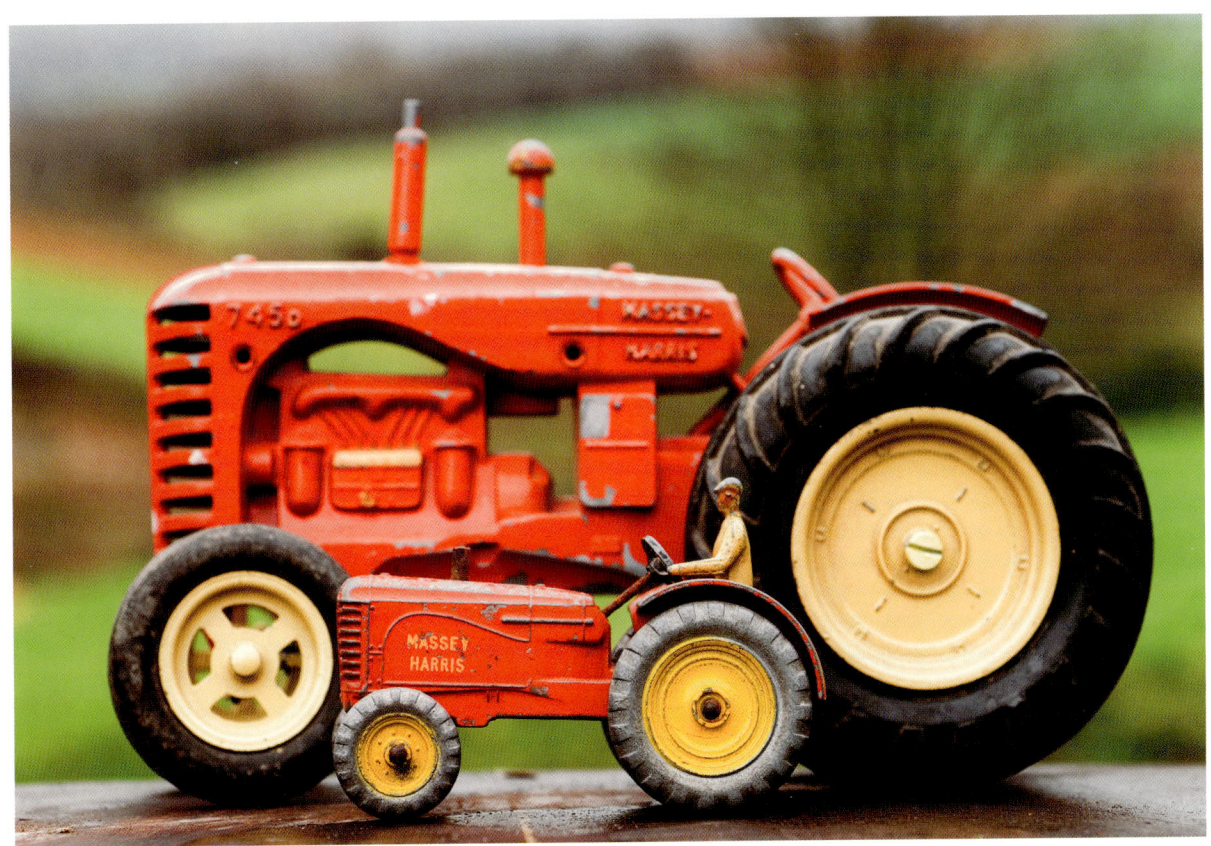

The neat garden roller is a delightful little model that will please all who love to play with Dinky Toys.

Garden Roller, 1948-58.

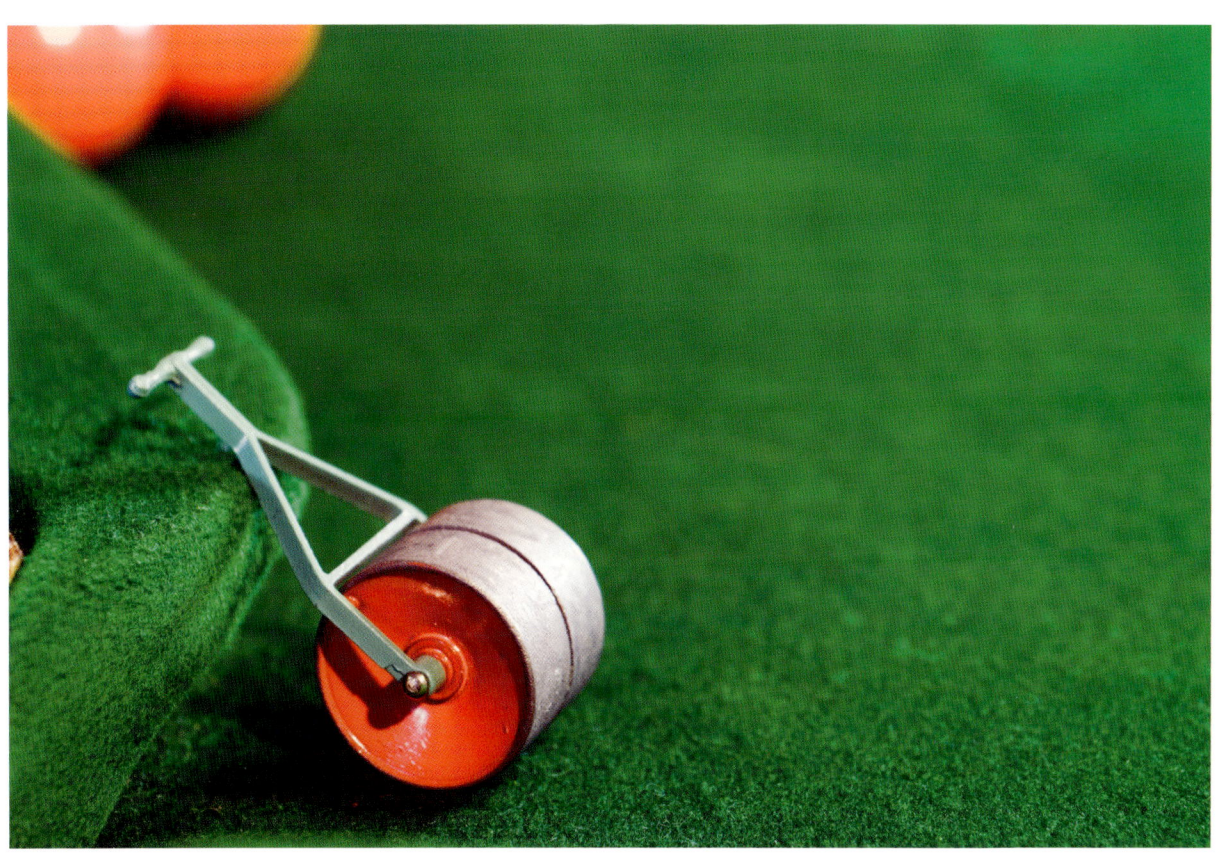

Aveling Barford Road Roller, 1948-63.

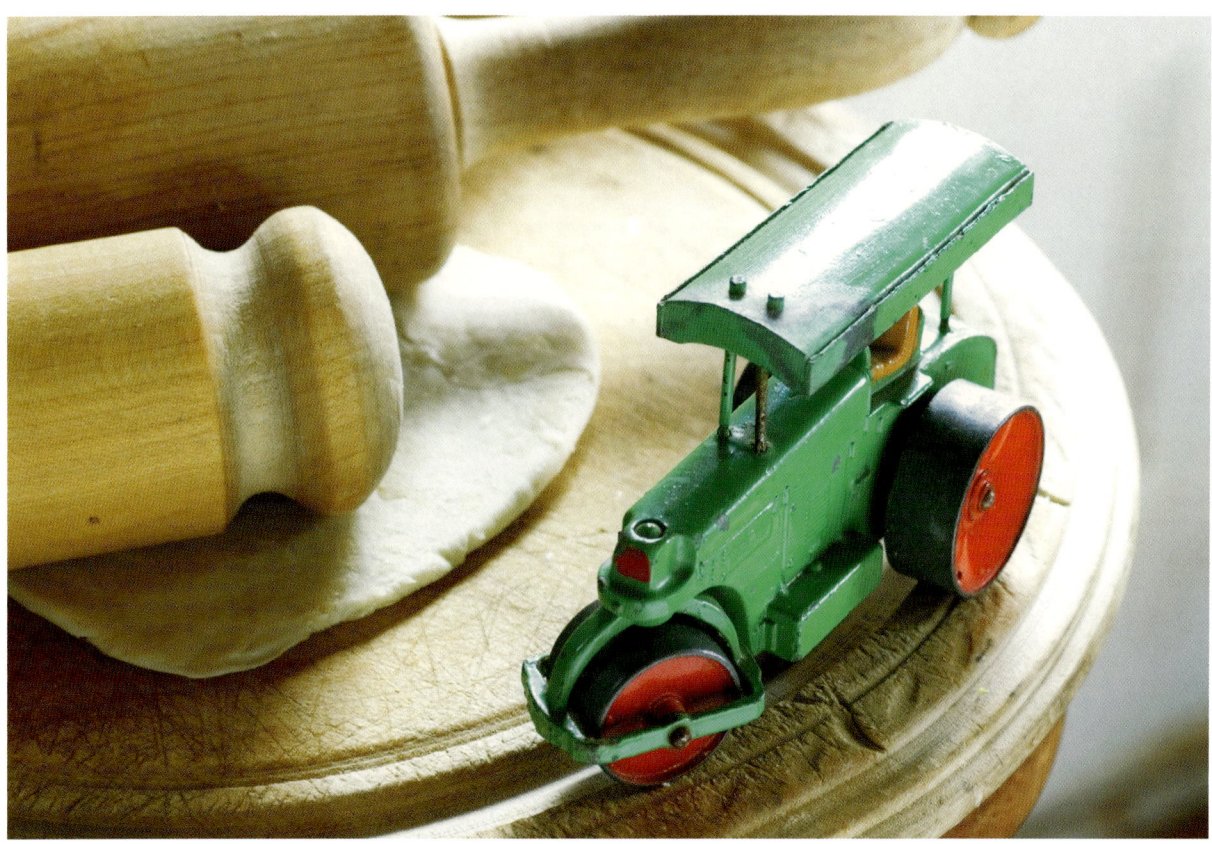

This model has sliding covers, tipping mechanism and opening rear door.

Bedford Refuse Wagon, 1948-64.

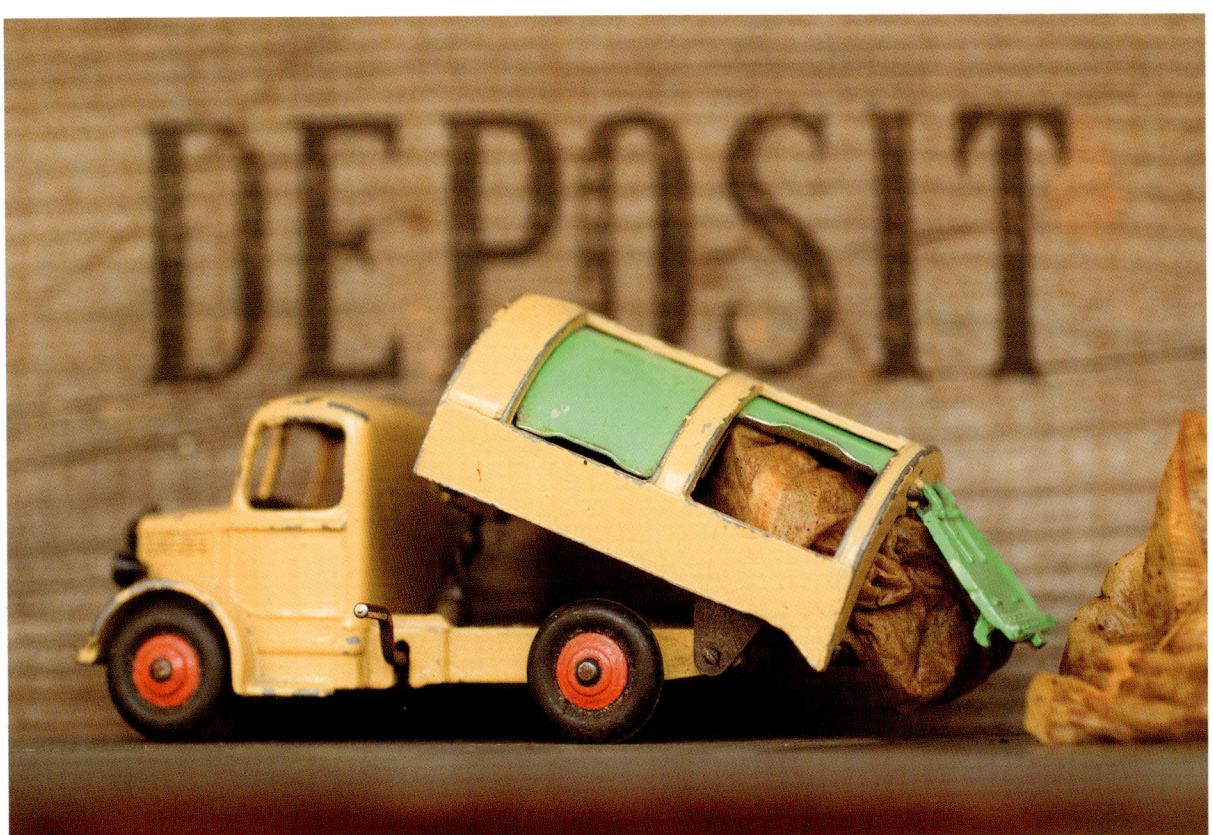

Seaplane 63B, 1945-57.
Re-issue as part of pre-war Mayo Composite Aircraft.

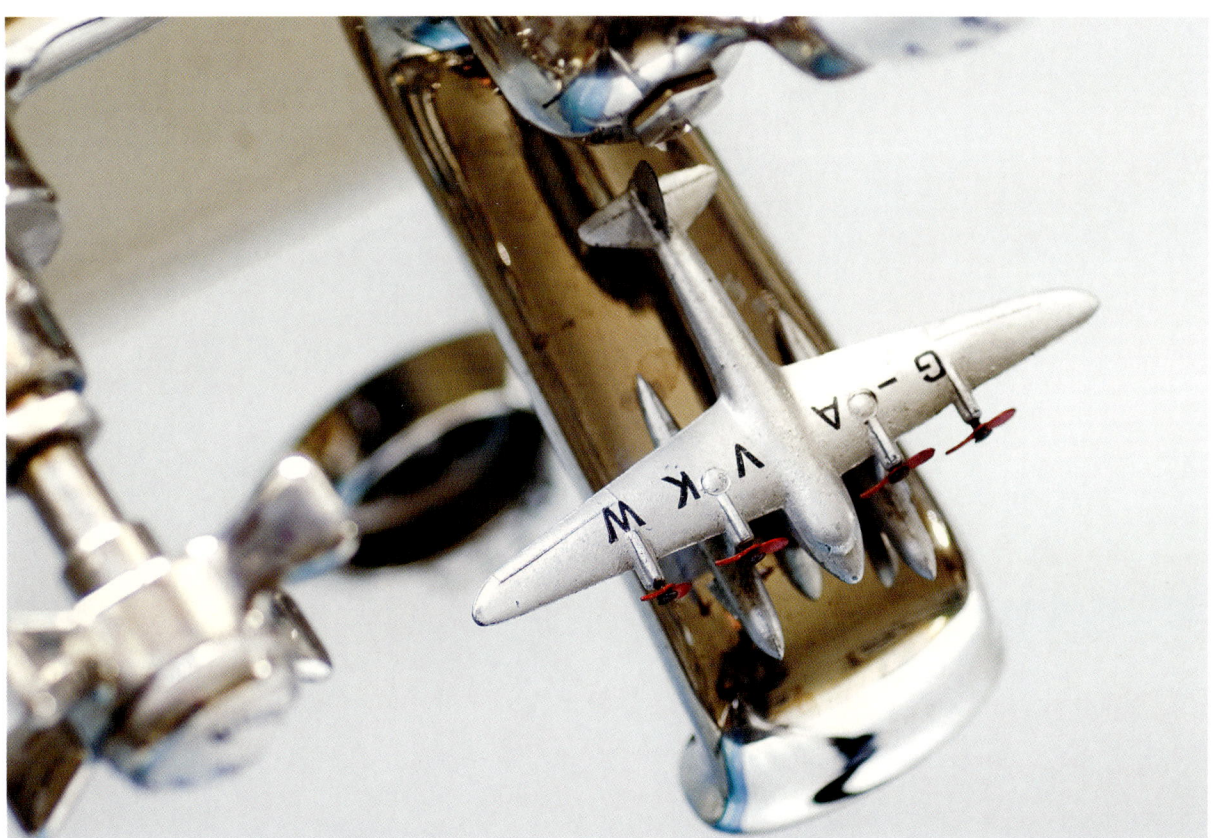

A striking model, one of the latest British Transport Aircraft.

Avro York Airliner, 1940-59.
Sharing the same parts as the Lancaster Bomber, the
Avro York Airliner was put to more domestic use.

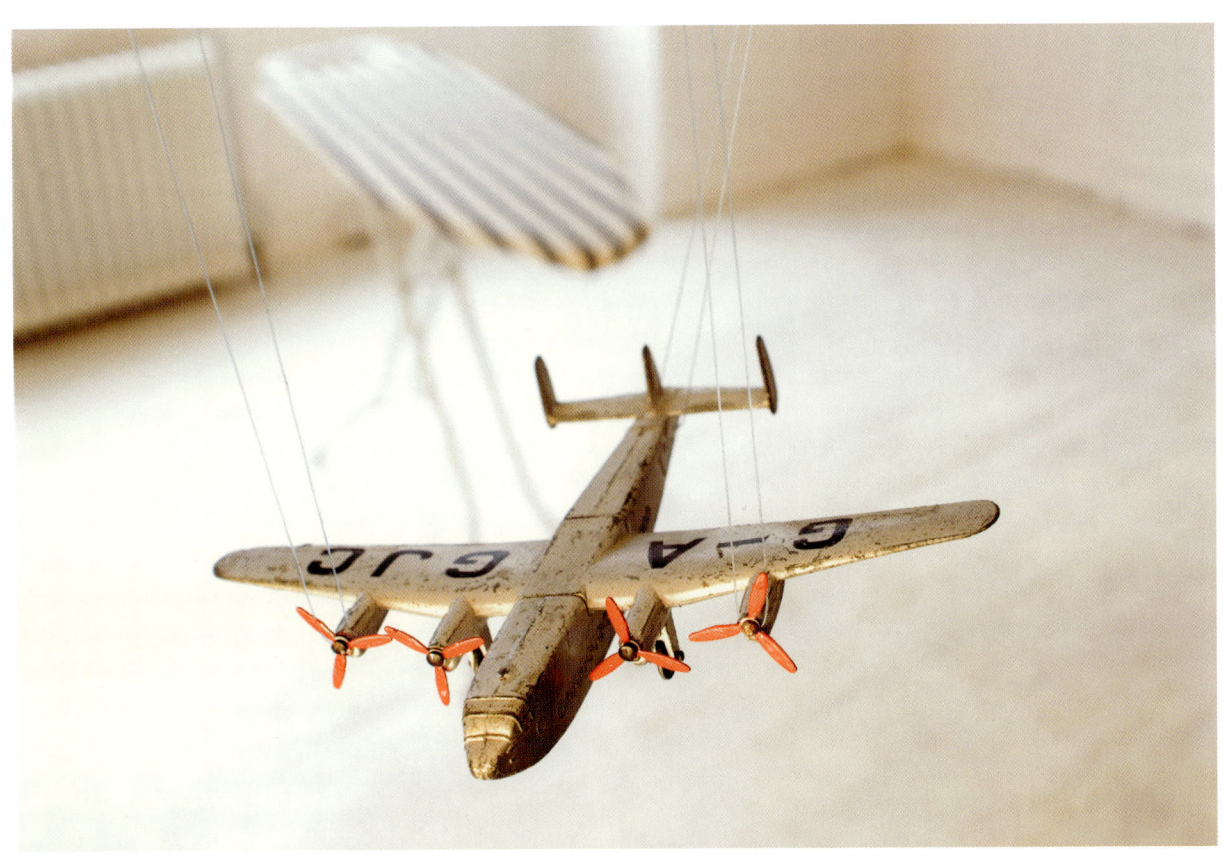

Cunard White Star Line, Queen Mary, 1934-49.
Re-issue of pre-war model.

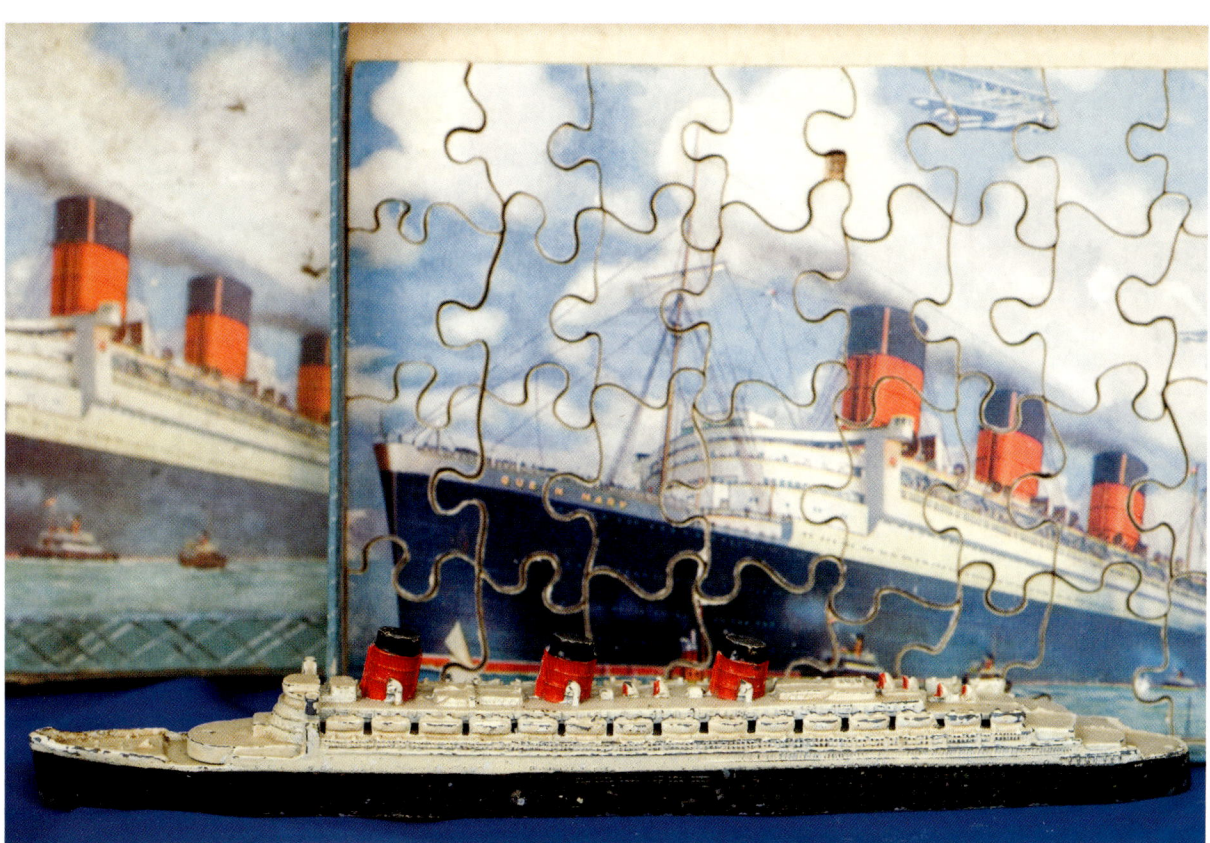

*A handsome model of a motor coach, giving
passengers good views in all directions.*

Single Deck Buses, 1948-52.

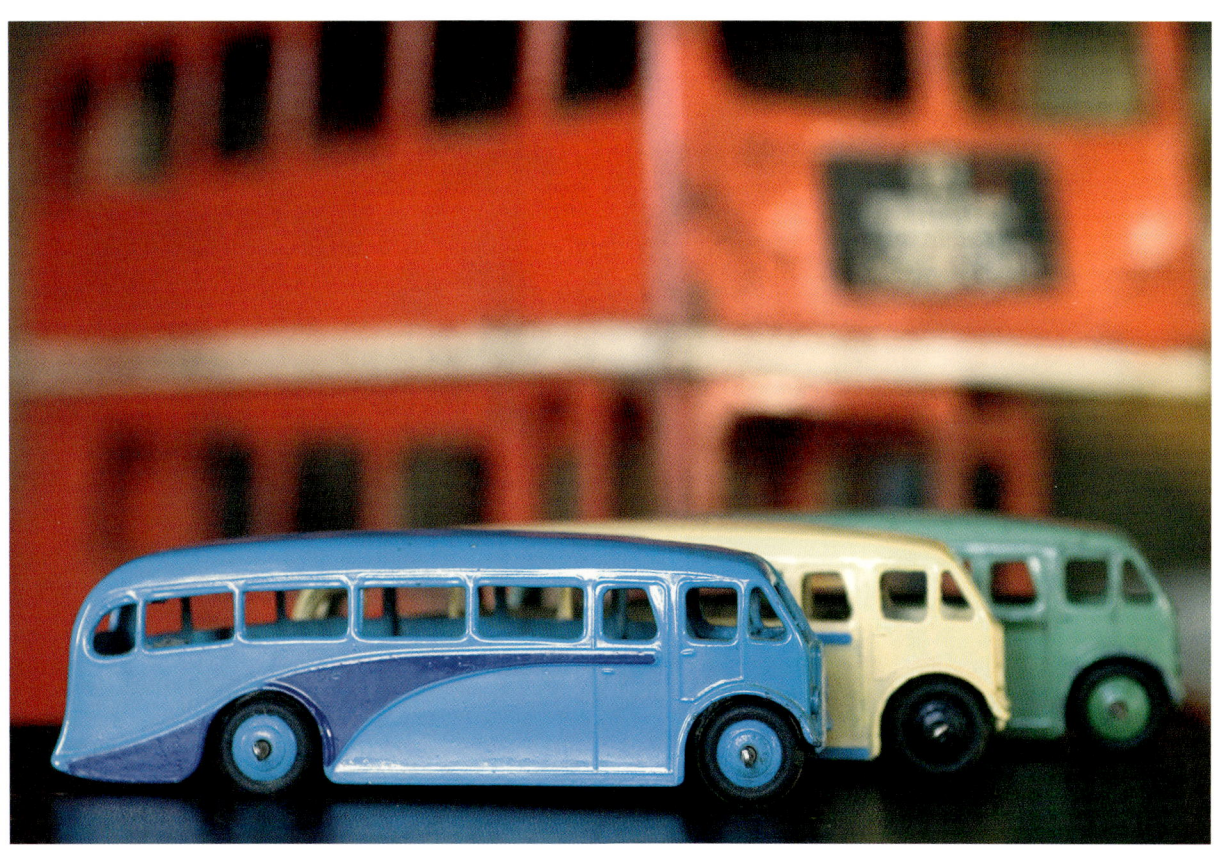

Fitted with detachable rubber tyres.

Taxi with driver, 1937-50.
Re-issue of pre-war model.

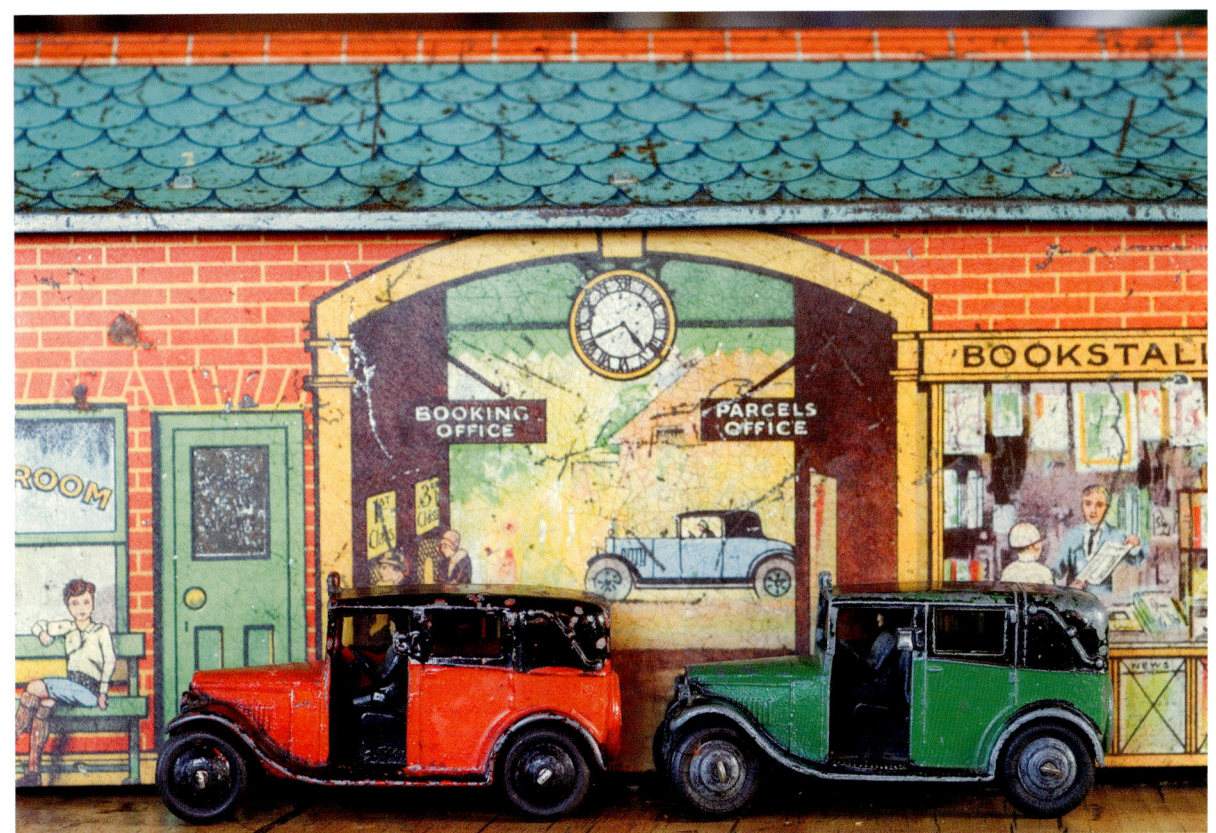

AA Motorcycle Patrol, 1935-63.
Re-issue of pre-war model.

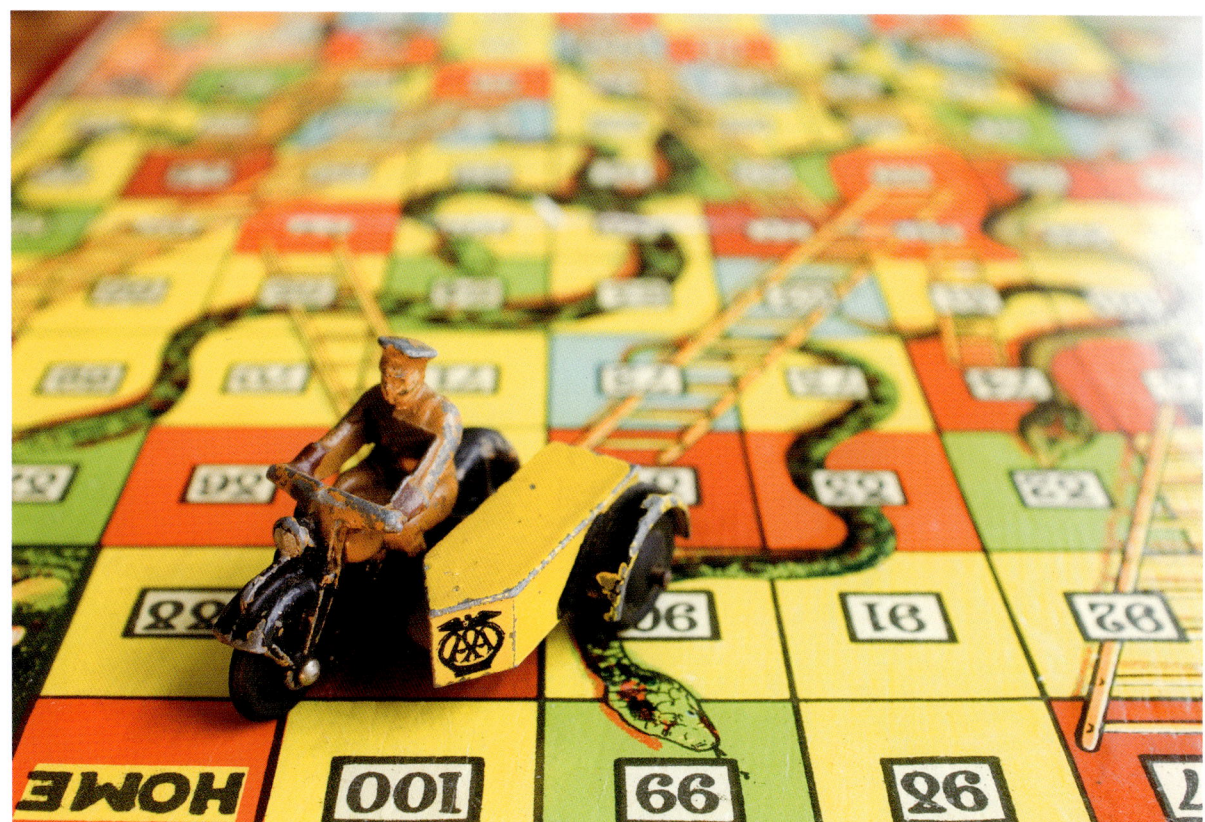

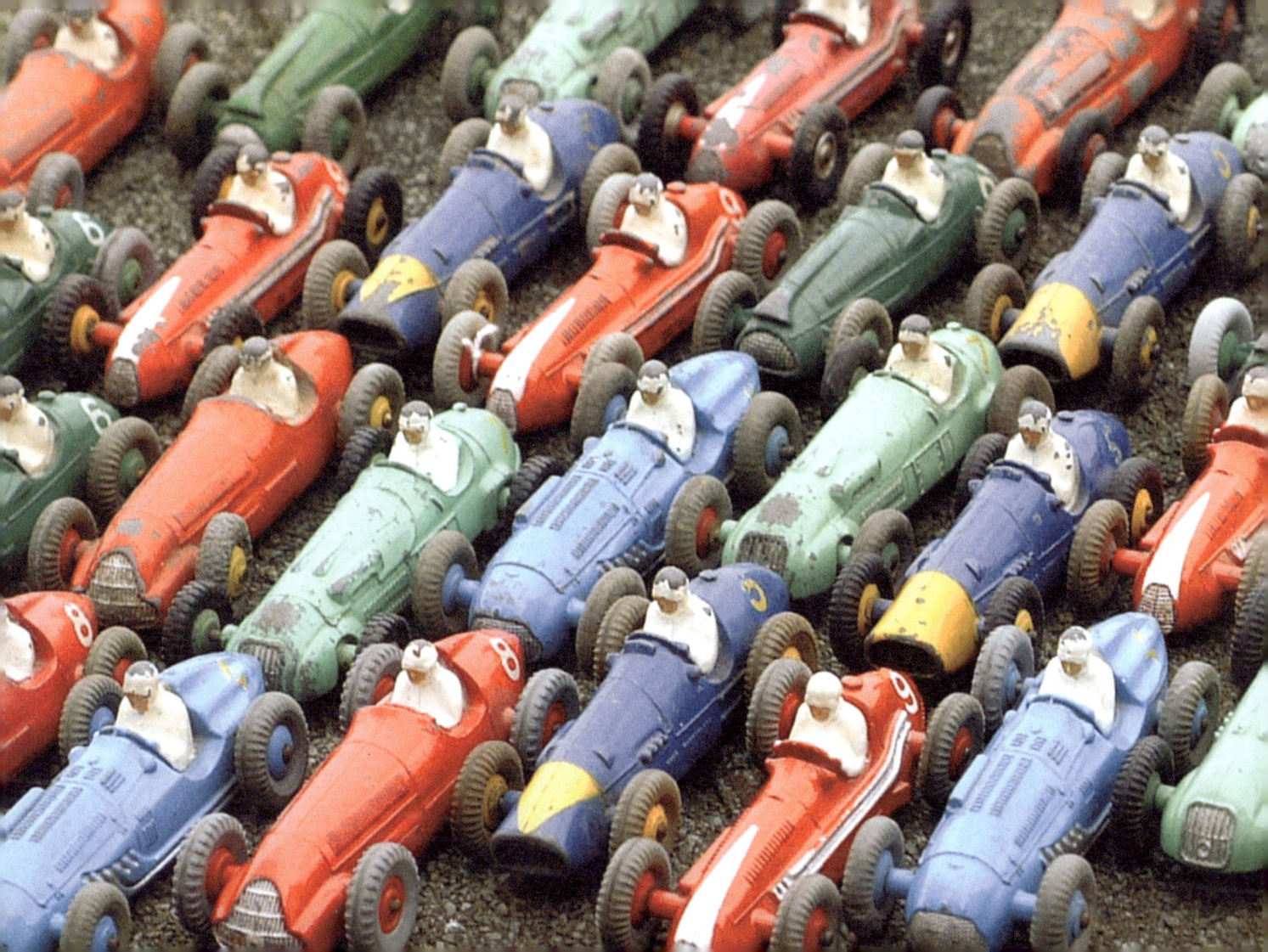